11/23

D1447939

The Strangest Way

The Strangest Way

Walking the Christian Path

Robert Barron

ORBIS BOOKS

Maryknoll, New York 10545

Founded in 1970, Orbis Books endeavors to publish works that enlighten the mind, nourish the spirit, and challenge the conscience. The publishing arm of the Maryknoll Fathers and Brothers, Orbis seeks to explore the global dimensions of the Christian faith and mission, to invite dialogue with diverse cultures and religious traditions, and to serve the cause of reconciliation and peace. The books published reflect the views of their authors and do not represent the official position of the Maryknoll Society. To learn more about Maryknoll and Orbis Books, please visit our website at www.maryknoll.org.

Copyright © 2002 by Robert Barron

Published by Orbis Books, Maryknoll, New York, U.S.A.

Manufactured in the United States of America

Library of Congress Cataloging-in-Publication Data

Barron, Robert E., 1959-
    The strangest way : walking the Christian path / Robert Barron.
        p.   cm.
    Includes bibliographical references.
    ISBN 1-57075-408-X (pbk.)
    1. Christian life – Catholic authors.   I. Title.
BX2350.3 .B375 2002
248.4 – dc21
                                                    2002000621

Contents

Acknowledgments

I would like to thank a number of people who supported, encouraged, and prayed for me during the writing of this book: Stanley Hauerwas, a man of both great tenacity and great generosity; Fr. Wayne Prist, like Barnabas, a son of encouragement; Fr. Paul Murray, O.P., preacher and spiritual master extraordinaire, who gave me the title for this book; and Fr. Stephen Grunow, a combination of John of the Cross and Karl Barth, who read the manuscript with care and always kept me on the beam.

Preface

Strange Christianity

*You know something's happening here
but you don't know what it is
do you, Mr. Jones?*
— BOB DYLAN

*We preach Christ crucified,
a stumbling block to Jews and a folly to Gentiles.*
— 1 Cor. 1:23

In 1996 there was a gathering of Christians and Buddhists at the monastery of Our Lady of Gethsemani in Kentucky. At the meeting were scholars and monks from both traditions, as well as the Dalai Lama himself. After days of intense conversation and shared prayer, one of the Buddhist participants spoke to an urgent point. What had been bothering him throughout the conference was the prominent display, in almost every room of the monastery, of a suffering man pinioned to a cross. To his mind, the crucifix represented the agony to which the meditation and practices of his religion were the solution. And thus, he asked his Christian interlocutors, what precisely was the point in showing this terrible scene over and over again? Those who were there say that this question — blunt, direct, and challenging — changed the tenor of the meeting for the better, forcing representatives of both sides to cut to the heart of the matter.

I love that man's question. More to the point, I love the *bother* that prompted it. Christians have become so accustomed to see-

9

ing the crucifix — in churches, in schools, on seasonal greeting
cards, worn as jewelry around people's necks — that they have
long since lost any sense of how awful and strange it is. But to the
first Christians, the cross of Christ was that and more. Paul called it
"a stumbling block to the Jews and foolishness to Gentiles" (1 Cor.
1:23), insinuating that it was sure to bother just about everybody.
For the first several centuries of Christianity, artists were reluctant
to depict the death of the Lord, because it was just too terrible.
They felt, perhaps, something of what that Buddhist commentator
at Gethsemani felt. And yet, Paul can say, "we proclaim Christ
crucified" (1 Cor. 1:23), and the entire Christian tradition — from
Augustine, to Francis of Assisi, to Dante, to Ignatius of Loyola, to
Trappist monks in the hills of Kentucky — has echoed him. Somehow, they knew, that writhing figure, pinned to his cross, *is* the
whole story.

There is a painting of the awful death of Jesus that the German
artist Matthias Grünewald completed in 1484 for the patients and
staff at a hospital specializing in diseases of the skin. It is one of the
most terribly beautiful depictions of Calvary ever made. The two
greatest Protestant theologians of the twentieth century — Paul
Tillich and Karl Barth — had a reproduction of this masterpiece
over their desks as they worked on their dogmatics. The body of
Grünewald's Jesus had been, it is obvious, impressive and powerful,
but now it is wracked, twisted, and disfigured — the neck at an
almost impossible angle to the torso, the hands and feet distended,
the legs bowed almost to the point of breaking, the chest covered in
wounds, scratches, and blisters, the head wreathed in a particularly
brutal crown of thorns. What is, for me, most disturbing are the
shut eyes and the gaping mouth: this Christ is no longer seeing
or speaking; he is simply lost in the terror of the moment. To the
right of the crucified Christ stands John the Baptist performing his
usual iconic task of pointing at the Lord, but what is remarkable
are the contortions in his arm, hand, and fingers as he indicates
the Christ. It is as though his own life has to be twisted into a new
and unusual form if he is to function effectively as a prophet of the
suffering Jesus.

When I was coming of age as a postconciliar Catholic, great stress was placed on Christianity's outreach to the modern world and to other religions. In accordance with this emphasis, Christianity's distinctive qualities and bright colors tended to be muted and its rough edges smoothed, while points of contact and continuity with the non-Christian and secular realms were consistently brought into the light and celebrated. As a result, the Christianity into which I was initiated was relatively bland and domesticated, easy to grasp and unthreatening.

Then, in the course of my formal theological education, I began to read the mystics, saints, and scholars of the classical Christian tradition. What I encountered there took my breath away. Whatever this Christian phenomenon was, it was certainly not the beige system of thought that had been presented to me. Rather it seemed to me the strangest, most exotic, surprising, and uncanny of all of the religious paths I had encountered. For at the very center of it is what the Buddhist scholar at Gethsemani and Matthias Grünewald saw with such clarity: a God who comes after us with a reckless abandon, breaking open his own heart in love in order to include us in the rhythm of his own life. Christianity, I saw, was not our disciplined quest for God, but God's relentless quest for us — even to the point of death. God died in order that we might be his friends. Whatever you think of that last statement, whether you deem it true, false, or nonsensical, the one thing it is not is bland; the one thing it is not saying is what everyone else is saying.

And friendship with God — not simply worship, discipleship, seeking, or ethical uprightness — but real intimacy with God entailed, I discovered, a giving of self that mirrored the radicality of God's own gift of self in Christ. The point of the Christian life is to be holy with the very holiness of God, and this means conformity with a love unto death. On both the human and divine side, therefore, there is a radical, even disquieting extremism about Christianity, and the best spirits in the Christian tradition do nothing to soften it; on the contrary, they intensify it.

It is this strange way that I wish to explore in the course of this book. My purpose is not so much apologetic as expository,

that is to say, I am interested, not primarily in making arguments
in support of Christianity, as in presenting Christianity in its odd
particularity. Accordingly, my target audience is my fellow Christians, perhaps especially those members of my own generation who
came of age during a rather beige time, though I would hope too
that non-Christians and nonbelievers would find much to ponder
in these pages. The philosopher Wittgenstein famously urged his
overly rational colleagues: "Don't think. Look!" My approach here
is Wittgensteinian. I want to show the Christian way as it is displayed on three distinctive paths and to invite my reader to look,
or better, to walk. I will use numerous and diverse sources in my
work of exposition: poetry, drama, painting, theology, spirituality,
architecture, philosophy, lives of the saints, and literature.

In the introduction, I will argue that Christianity is not so much
a system of thought or set of convictions as a path or series of practices. Like baseball, philosophy, or being an American, it is a whole
pattern of life. I will also explore the typically modern assumptions
that led us away from a practiced Christianity to the attenuated
form that I encountered as a young man. Then in the next three
chapters, I will present the paths that constitute the Christian way:
finding the center, knowing you are a sinner, and realizing your life
is not about you. At the heart of each of these chapters will be
a literary display of the path, the first taken from Evelyn Waugh's
Brideshead Revisited, the second from Dante's *Purgatorio,* and the
third from Flannery O'Connor's *The Violent Bear It Away.* And
each chapter will conclude with a presentation of a set of concrete
practices designed to keep one close to the path in question.

If it is not already obvious from these literary choices, I am a
Roman Catholic, and this book has, unapologetically, a Catholic
flavor and orientation. But I have always retained a deep sympathy
for C. S. Lewis's project of recovering "mere" Christianity, that is,
the essential core of a classical Christian faith shared by all of the
churches, Catholic, Protestant, and Orthodox. It is my ecumenical
hope that Christians of all stripes and styles could profit from these
meditations on walking the strange way of the Lord.

Introduction

Paths and Practices

Don't think. Look!

—Ludwig Wittgenstein

Bridges once wrote Gerard Manley Hopkins and asked him to tell him how he, Bridges, could believe. Bridges was an agnostic. Hopkins wrote back, "Give alms." —Flannery O'Connor

Come and see.

—John 1:39

Prelude: Apprenticeship

One of the earliest terms used to describe Christianity is the simple but evocative word "way" (Acts 9:2). This signals something of great importance: Christianity, before all else, is a form of life, a path that one walks. It is way of seeing, a frame of mind, an attitude, but more than this, it is a manner of moving and acting, standing and relating. It is not simply a matter of the mind but of the body as well. In fact, one could say that Christianity is not real until it has insinuated itself into the blood and the bones, until it becomes an instinct, as much physical as spiritual. Perhaps the most direct description is this: Christianity, the way of Jesus Christ, is a culture, a style of life supported by a unique set of convictions, assumptions, hopes, and practices. It is like a game with a distinctive texture, feel, and set of rules. As such, it is a milieu into which one must be introduced through a process of practice and *apprenticeship*.

When a young man came to a Renaissance painter in order to

learn the craft of painting, he moved in with the master, watching him at close quarters, catching the rhythms of his movements and the overall pattern of his life. In time, he might be given a simple task to perform — say the crushing of pigments — and this he would do for many months or even years. Though he undoubtedly found the process tedious and longed to involve himself in the actual painting of a great canvas, the young man did his job and thereby learned, not only the rudiments of color but more importantly the patience and discipline required for the production of a work of art. Only gradually would he be initiated into the more complex dimensions of the artist's realm of activity: draftsmanship, composition, application of color, use of *chiaroscuro,* the depiction of philosophical and mythological themes. During this entire process, he would scrupulously follow the direction and style of his master who, in his youth, had learned the same techniques from his elders. Only at the end of his years-long training, having moved, body and spirit, into the milieu of the painter, would the novice perhaps develop his own approach, find his own path.

And something very similar unfolds when a child steps onto a baseball diamond to begin his initiation into the game. His coach moves him through a series of drills — throwing, catching, swinging the bat, fielding the ball — designed to place the requisite skills of baseball into his muscles and mind. When necessary, the master of the game might demonstrate with his own body the pivot or slide that he wants the novice to make. If he is imaginative, the coach invites his charges to watch videos of great baseball players, encouraging them to mimic the graceful swing of Ted Williams or the energetic baserunning of Roberto Clemente. He might introduce them to the lore of the game, relating stories of the 1976 World Series or the Yankees' 1927 season; he might pass on the wisdom and strategies of successful managers like Tony LaRussa and Leo Durocher, and he might share the goofy eloquence of Casey Stengel. At the end of this process of apprenticeship, the young man, it is hoped, will see and think and move as a baseball player — and he will love the entire form of life that is baseball.

When I was nineteen, I entered an accelerated program in philosophy at Catholic University in Washington, D.C. This was the beginning of my apprenticeship to a whole series of masters and my entry into a world that I still find enchanting. One of my professors in the first year of the program required us all to write a two-page paper each week on a single argument from a Platonic dialogue. His critiques were ruthless and his grading was draconian: he would return these papers (which we thought ranked with the classics of Western thought), and they were covered with lines, question marks, exclamation points registering his shock, corrections of grammar, and, hovering over all of it, a desperately low grade. One of his commonest remarks was "you are just repeating standard arguments here; you are not *philosophizing*." What exactly philosophizing was none of us knew for sure, but the master's criticisms and humiliations were compelling us to find out.

In another seminar, a classmate of mine finished his ninety-minute critical presentation on the *Nicomachean Ethics* of Aristotle with the following rhetorical flourish: "What then are we to do with this text?" The professor, an avid Aristotelian, responded with devastating laconicism, "Perhaps we could read it more carefully." Once more, we were all being taught how to philosophize through a sort of *via negativa*, seeing precisely how *not* to approach a great thinker. In my final year, I took a course that bore the improbable title "The Analogy and Univocity of Being in the Middle Ages." About twenty of us met on Monday nights with a gentle genius whose native language, according to local legend, was Latin. Under his guidance we worked our way through the untranslated texts of Thomas Aquinas on this obscure but important issue in medieval epistemology, learning thereby an arcane and fascinating argot that linked us to our distant ancestors in the philosophical tradition.

The most memorable moment for me in the process of apprenticeship took place midway through my second year. After spending several months studying the issue of human freedom and divine foreknowledge, I raised a challenging question one day in class. My professor gave a brief response that I found inadequate, and I pursued the issue. Looking at me with a combination of delight and surprise, he said, "Okay, make your case." With some trepidation, knowing that the entire class was listening avidly, I then began to philosophize — not so much commenting, learning, analyzing, but thinking on my own, following the argument where it led. Sensing my excitement, the professor kept guiding me, spurring me on with questions and comments. Suddenly, I was not studying a Platonic dialogue; I was in one, the teacher playing patient Socrates to my enthusiastic Thrasymachus. In that moment, still fresh in my memory all these years later, I entered, however tentatively and imperfectly, into the great conversation of Western philosophy; in the course of that exchange, I became a brother, however unworthy, to Parmenides, Augustine, Aquinas, Hobbes, and Kant.

In the course of those three years I entered a new world. At the end of the program, I had, not simply new ideas and information, but new eyes and a new mind. I spoke a different language and related to my environment in a discernibly novel way. Those who knew me before my philosophical initiation realized that, afterward, something was radically and irreversibly changed in me. That is what a true apprenticeship does: it converts you.

The first words spoken by Jesus in the Gospel of John are addressed to two former disciples of John the Baptist: "What are you looking for" (John 1:38)? They respond, somewhat surprisingly, "Where are you staying?" One might expect that, in the presence of this new rabbi, they would have answered, "the truth" or "enlightenment" or "peace." Instead, they answer the question elliptically with another question — and this odd nonanswer is, in fact, the key to the exchange. What they seek, what they want to know, is not so much the teaching or wisdom or perspective of the rabbi; they want to know *him*, more to the point, precisely where and how he lives. In the mystical vocabulary of John's Gospel, the verb *menein* (stay or remain) refers to the source of one's life and meaning. Thus, Jesus says that he *remains* with the Father, drawing his being from him, and he promises that he and the Father will *remain* with believers, feeding and nurturing them. Therefore, in asking where he "stays," the disciples are wondering about the form of life that sustains him, the source of his power. Obviously pleased by their response, Jesus says encouragingly, "Come and see" (John 1:39). And then, John tells us, "they came and saw where he was staying, and they remained with him that day." In this simple and understated narrative, we see that the form of Christian discipleship is not primarily listening or learning but rather moving into the "house" of Jesus, discerning his mode of life, being with him at close quarters.

After this visit with the rabbi from Nazareth, one of the disciples — now identified as Andrew — emerges with enthusiasm, running to his brother Simon and exclaiming, "We have found the Messiah" (John 1:41). It seems clear that the body (staying with him) in a significant sense conditions the mind ("he is the Messiah"), the way of life shaping the conviction. Throughout his ministry, Jesus certainly teaches his disciples, but the instruction always takes place in the far more elemental context of *following* him, as though the learning would never take place uncoupled from the life. In a word, Jesus invites his friends into an apprenticing relationship with him, encouraging them to "catch" his way of being through proximity, imitation, and love. And the processes that we traced in our examples above — practicing, watching patiently, repeating, disciplining the body — are all at work as one is grafted onto Christ.

The way of Jesus has, over the centuries, given rise to myriad expressions in theology, liturgy, architecture, poetry, ethics, and spirituality. Staying with Jesus has resulted in the *Summa theologiae* of Thomas Aquinas, the *Divine Comedy* of Dante, Cologne Cathedral, the life of St. Antony of the Desert, the silence and suffering of John of the Cross, and the radical nonviolence of Dorothy Day. What can be lost or forgotten is the connection of all of these to the originating apprenticeship, to the form of life from which they flowed. Thus, Dorothy Day's protest against a culture predicated upon militarism arose, not simply from her reflection, but from the conditioning of her body through a lifetime of spiritual exercises; and Thomas Aquinas said explicitly that the depth of his theological analysis came, not so much from the acuity of his mind, as from the intensity of his prayer. Both Dorothy and Thomas were disciples who had "come and seen"; both had stayed with the Master and learned, through practice, a new way of being in the world.

The Problem with Modernity

I have been dwelling on this embodied and distinctive character of Christianity precisely because I fear that, in recent years, it has been largely lost sight of. The culture which is Christianity, the sacred way, expressed in movement, practice and apprenticeship, has become too often a faint echo of the secular culture or a privatized and individualized set of convictions. The dense texture of the Christian way has been worn thin, and its bright colors allowed to bleed into beige, and this attenuating has been due to an accommodation to the characteristically modern frame of mind. Whether born of a desire to imitate the modern world or a hope to reach out to it in a missionary spirit, this accommodationism has, I maintain, robbed Christianity of its persuasiveness and spiciness.

Every year a group of students from the seminary at which I teach makes a lengthy pilgrimage to the Holy Land. Their sojourn usually coincides with the Muslim penitential month of Ramadan. What strikes these American Catholic seminarians is how unavoidable, vivid, and "in your face" the practice of Ramadan is. Simply to walk outside one's residence and open one's eyes and ears is to know that something powerful is going on. Ramadan affects the way the people behave, move, gesture, do business, eat, and celebrate (one seminarian was especially impressed by the festiveness at the end of the month of fasting, which trumps any Fourth of July celebration he had ever experienced). The rhetorical questions that I have posed to my students when they share these impressions are the following: If a foreign visitor came to largely Catholic Chicago during our penitential season of Lent, would that person notice anything in particular? Would it be obvious in any sense that something of religious significance was underway? Would you see Lent in people's faces, bodies, movements? Does it change the way they buy and sell, advertise, eat and sleep? The answer to all of these questions is, alas, no. And that is the problem. What does indeed affect our bodies, what does mark the way we move and sleep and do business, what has profoundly written itself into our muscles and bones, is the modern ethos, the secular religion. And a beige, bland, attenuated Christianity is no match for such a powerful and focused adversary. Very true - freedom ? ?

To understand this phenomenon of the deculturalization of Christianity, we must consider, however briefly, the thought of the man generally regarded as the founder of modernity, René Descartes. In his groundbreaking and hugely influential *Discourse on Method*, Descartes lays out the program that has formed the culture that, in turn, has shaped most of us. Surveying the history of philosophical and religious thought, Descartes despairs of finding any coherency, consistency, or certitude. Whereas mathematics has remained impressively stable over the centuries, metaphysics and philosophy are a jumble of conflicting opinions, varying starting points, elemental disagreements. The greatest minds — Plato, Aristotle, Cicero, Thomas Aquinas — are at odds with each other and, worse yet, there seems no common ground on the basis of which to adjudicate their disputes. Classical philosophy, in short, is like an old seaside city, full of winding streets, dead-ends, collapsing buildings, and blind alleys — an ugly and dangerous place. Would it not be a desideratum, Descartes reasons, simply to tear down the old town, find a firmer construction site, and start afresh, this time under the guidance of one architect with a grand, unifying plan?[1]

The wrecking-ball our philosopher chooses is the powerful one of systematic doubt: if a proposition or conviction *can* be doubted, it *should* be doubted. So avid is Descartes to discover philosophical *terra firma* that he swings this ball wildly, knocking over every idea, principle, experience, and assumption — save one. He finds that the one thing he cannot doubt is that he is doubting; the one thing the wrecking ball cannot knock over is itself. This intuition is expressed in what is certainly the most famous one-liner in the history of philosophy: *cogito ergo sum*, I think therefore I am.[2] In this luminously "clear and distinct" idea, utterly incapable of being doubted or thought away, Descartes has found his starting point, his foundation. Not in nature, not in the tradition, not in conversation, but in the private interiority of his consciousness, he has discovered the rock upon which he can confidently build his new modern city of thought.

And the unified plan for the construction is a purely rational, mathematical method consisting of four steps: (1) begin with clear and distinct ideas, (2) break problems down into their component parts, (3) move from one step to another in a chain of reasoning only when logic compels such a move, and (4) rigorously check your work.[3] Beginning with the *cogito* and following the *méthode*, the Cartesian philosopher will design a safe, clean, orderly, and rationally satisfying system; the philosopher will build a "modern" philosophical city, happily unlike the untidy and confusing town of classical thought.

Now this Cartesian approach — subjectivist, rationalist, suspicious — had an enormous influence, not only on the shaping of the modern physical sciences, but also on the emergence of a typically modern understanding of religion. When Immanuel Kant, at the end of the eighteenth century, sought to articulate a religion "within the limits of reason alone," he appealed to the luminous inner conviction of the moral imperative. All of religion — liturgy, ritual, biblical narrative, dogmas, creeds — can and should be reduced to this subjective sense that we must follow our ethical duty.[4] And when Friedrich Schleiermacher, at the very beginning of the nineteenth century, endeavored to defend Christianity against its "cultured despisers," he did so on the basis of the purportedly universal experience of being absolutely dependent.[5] Again, everything else in the world of faith is reducible to that grounding mystical intuition. In short, both thinkers made a typically Cartesian appeal to a clear and distinct *subjective* starting point for the religious. Kant and Schleiermacher find an echo in two of the most influential twentieth-century theologians, Paul Tillich and Karl Rahner. For Tillich, Christianity is grounded in a sense of being "ultimately concerned," that is to say, pressed upon by the unconditioned power of being itself.[6] And for Rahner, faith rests on the individual's experience of standing in the presence of the absolute mystery, which conditions and lures all particular acts of knowing and willing.[7] Interior, subjective experience is the religious *terra firma*, the rock upon which the whole structure is built.

In the popular Christianity of the last thirty years, this subjectivist bias has been plainly evident. In catechetics, theological reflection, liturgy, and parish ministry, a great stress has been placed on "experience," one's inner sense of the presence and activity of God. "Recall a time when you felt close to God" or "remember a moment when you were sure of God's forgiveness" have been standard starting points for religious instruction and formation. And biblical texts, doctrines, liturgical formulas have tended to be read in light of those private experiences, as though the experiences constituted the criterion of faith, the final court of appeal.

Descartes's anti-traditionalism, his prejudice against cluttered old intellectual towns, also had a decisive influence on modern thought. One of the hallmarks of Enlightenment philosophy and science is the gleeful — and sometimes manic — questioning of received traditions and revered authorities. In his programmatic essay "What Is Enlightenment?" Kant expresses the Cartesian idea under the rubric of the metaphor of coming of age.[8] He tells European intellectuals that they had been behaving like children but that the moment of their majority has arrived: we celebrate "man's emergence from his self-incurred immaturity." Here the tradition is not the confusing and dangerous old city, but rather the nursery school or the playground, the place where children remain subject to arbitrary authority. It is long past time, Kant insists, for European thinkers to move out of the comfortable but infantilizing confines of this intellectual kindergarten and, in his famous phrase, "dare to know."

In his *Essence of Christianity*, a paradigmatically modern text, Adolf von Harnack gave powerful expression to this Kantian imperative. Scraping centuries of traditions and practices away, like so many barnacles on the hull of a ship, Harnack presented Christianity as a simple moral system and Christ, not as the Son of God, but as a humble ethical teacher. Liturgy, the dogmatic tradition, rituals, metaphysics — all of it was seen as peripheral to, even ultimately obscuring of, these core Christian facts. We see something similar in Paul Tillich's early work in dogmatic theology. Convinced that many traditional Christian ideas have become unintelligible, Tillich sought to redefine them in terms of our psychological experience. Thus God becomes "that which unconditionally concerns us" and the Incarnation is "the appearance of the new being under the conditions of estrangement."[9]

The Cartesian cleansing project was perhaps no more dramatically evident than in much of Catholic liturgical theology in the years just prior to the Second Vatican Council. In many ways, the work of Josef Jungmann is paradigmatic here. This extremely influential thinker held that almost all of the liturgical developments since the time of Charlemagne amounted to so much clutter, obscuring the pristine beauty of the church's house of prayer. Accordingly, he recommended (and his recommendation was widely heeded) a cleansing return to the simplicity of the patristic liturgy and ritual. It is instructive that Jungmann employed the very Cartesian metaphor of the cluttered house in need of purification and not, say, John Henry Newman's image of the developing plant requiring occasional pruning.[10] Once again, tradition was construed rather one-sidedly as obscuring rather than as illuminating.

One would not have to look far to see this suspicion of tradition in the recent life of the church. For many years in Catholic circles an appeal to the broad tradition was seen as retrograde, dangerously "preconciliar." In popular articles, workshops, and homilies, the "new" theology was presented in sharp contrast to a usually caricatured "classical" version, this despite the fact that the great theological Fathers of the Council — de Lubac, Daniélou, Rahner — remained profoundly respectful of the tradition. There has seemed to reign in contemporary Christianity a sort of hermeneutic of suspicion with regard to traditional ecclesial practices and theological forms, a tendency to see them as a front for plays of power or systems of domination.

Descartes has shaped modernity in his subjectivism, his anti-traditionalism, and, perhaps most importantly, in his exaggerated rationalism. We saw that the foundation for Descartes's project is the *cogito*, the self-authenticating thinking subject guided by the mathematical method. Now precisely because all sense experience can be doubted, and because the body belongs to the realm of sense, this indubitable *ego* can have no necessary connection to the body. The source and ground of the characteristically modern philosophy therefore is literally disincarnate. Just as the Cartesian mind is removed from the environing tradition, so is it removed from muscle, bone, movement, and blood.

One can spot this body-spirit dualism in so much of modern philosophy. Thus Kant radically separates sensuousness from understanding in the *Critique of Pure Reason* and, in the *Foundations of the Metaphysics of Morals*, he drives a wedge between anthropology (empirical, culturally determined) and the categorical imperative (purely rational, universal, disembodied).[11] And in Hegel, we find a sharp distinction between religion on the one hand and true philosophy on the other, religion tainted by imagination and particularity and philosophy beautifully abstract and rational.[12]

This splitting of body and mind has shaped contemporary theology precisely in the measure that certain theologians have done their work apart from the discipline and practice of the believing community. Paul Tillich, for example, composed a massive three-volume systematic theology, while admitting that he rarely attended church service. Purely academic theologians — alone with their books, immersed in the intellectual tradition of Christianity, but not *practicing* their faith in any measurable way — are thinking in the disembodied Cartesian mode. When Hans Urs von Balthasar calls for a "kneeling theology" rather than a "sitting theology," he is assuming that intellectuals will theologize more accurately about Christianity when their minds are formed in the concrete (and very bodily) discipline of prayer and worship.[13]

And this Cartesian body/mind dualism is especially apparent in the texture of ordinary Christian life. In the last thirty years (especially in Catholicism), the bodily gestures and practices of the faith — rosaries, benedictions, processions, the performance of the works of mercy, devotions to the saints, novenas, pilgrimages, kneeling for prayer, the wearing of distinctive clothes — were largely set aside *and not replaced.* From the height of a typically Cartesian rationalism, such things were decried as superstitious, primitive, unworthy of properly enlightened Christians. In the years that I came of age as a Catholic — the late sixties and seventies — a terrible rationalism seemed to reign (though I'm sure the teachers and theologians of that time would have been surprised by such a description). What I mean is that there was a characteristically modern tendency to *explain* everything, to make our religion understandable and inoffensive. And among the principal casualities of this rationalism were the practices that appealed not so much to the mind as to the imagination and the body. Now what is a consequence of this disincarnate Christianity? A generation fascinated by "spirituality" and often bored by the church; millions embracing the colorful embodiments of the New Age and disdainful of the parlor-talk and learned squabbling of mainstream Christianity.

Back to Practices

In his early work, the twentieth-century philosopher Ludwig Wittgenstein tried to clean up the tangled garden of philosophy by laying bare the simple logical forms of propositions, effectively reducing language to mathematics.[14] How typically Cartesian! But in his puzzling and moving later writings, he described the futility of that earlier project. Now acutely aware that language can never be reduced univocally to one logical form, Wittgenstein began patiently to sift his way through the myriad and self-validating "games" of language that we play at various times and for various reasons. Words, he concluded, are like tools in a toolbox, used ad hoc, now for this purpose, now for that, or like chess pieces on a chessboard, moving according to certain fixed rules but in a variety of complicated ways, depending on context and circumstance.[15] And just as one learns what tools are by working with them and what rooks, queens, and bishops are by moving them in actual games of chess, so one learns a language by *using* it, playing it, hearing and speaking it. There is no one great form of speech that we can discern abstractly from the outside and then use as a universal criterion; rather, we must plow through the whole of language, attentive to subtle varieties in usage, barely perceptible shifts in the rules of the game. We know speech, not from a splendid and unique Cartesian height, but from the ground, plowing our way. In a word, we must become apprentices to the game of language, using and practicing it.

One of Wittgenstein's influences was the eighteenth-century German poet Wolfgang von Goethe. When practically every intellectual of his time was embracing the analytical rationalism of Newtonian science, Goethe resisted the tide. He complained that Newtonian experimenters subjected the things of nature too much to *their* intrusive gaze and questions, so that, armed with a few elementary principles, they set out to master the objects and movements of the cosmos. Newtonian science amounted to a placing of the world under the bright (and unattractive) light of aggressive human reason. What he proposed as an alternative was a far more contemplative and poetic method. If you want to understand the nature of a plant, Goethe reasoned, it is not advisable to rip it out of the ground, take it back to a laboratory, and dissect it. Following such a method, you will know certain data concerning the organism, but you will know practically nothing of the thing itself: how it develops, how it moves and grows, how it relates to its environment. It would be much more effective to sit with the plant, watch it as it unfolds, draw it, keep a log of its changes and reactions, in short, allowing it to ask and answer its own questions. What will happen, as one follows the Goethe method, is that the *world* of the plant will emerge, in all of its richness, unpredictability, and complexity.[16] And the Goethean scientist, by his patience and respectful practice, will garner a far deeper science of the plant than will his Newtonian counterpart, knowing it and not simply knowing about it.

A very good example of the Goethean method in action is the work of the zoologist Jane Goodall. She became convinced that

Western scientists knew little about apes and chimpanzees precisely because, in the Newtonian mode, they took them out of their proper environment and studied them in the extremely artificial setting of the zoo or laboratory. Accordingly, she endeavored to study these animals up close, living with them in *their* world, watching their movements and behaviors over a period of many years. In this way, Goodall uncovered many hitherto undiscovered facts about chimpanzees and effectively overturned many assumptions that had been based on hasty and impatient research. À la Goethe, she accepted the discipline of apprenticeship, allowing the animals' world itself to be her master, and à la Wittgenstein, she learned the chimps' "game" by playing it.

In the thirteenth century, Thomas Aquinas said that the soul is in the body, not as contained by it, but as containing it.[17] To make such an observation, one must stand radically outside of a Cartesian world of body/soul dualism. The soul, for Thomas, is not "in" or "next to" the body, a separable entity; rather the body is "in" the soul, implicated in it, marking and shaping it. Consequently, in Thomas's epistemology, there is nothing in the mind that does not enter through the senses, that is to say, through the concrete facticity of the body. We find an extremely interesting echo of Thomas Aquinas in the late nineteenth century in the psychological work of William James. Toward the end of his epoch-making text *The Principles of Psychology*, James makes a boldly anti-dualist remark concerning the nature of belief. Sometimes, he says, we come to conviction in a moment, through a flash of insight, but usually "our will can lead us to the same result by a very simple method: we need only in cold blood ACT as if the thing in question were real, and keep acting as if it were real, and it will infallibly end by growing into such a connection with our life that it will become real."[18] In other words, it is not the case that action (the moves of the body) always follow from conviction (the move of the mind); rather, it can proceed in precisely the opposite direction, action and desire shaping thought, literally *making* something real for the mind. For James, this is not acquiescing to "wishful thinking" but acknowledging that the will and, above all, the practices of the body play a decisive role in knowing. Soul, will, mind, and matter are inextricably intertwined, radically interdependent.

In 1871, John Henry Newman published *The Grammar of Assent*, a text that represents the culmination of Newman's lifelong wrestling with the problem of faith and reason, or, more precisely, how it is that we give assent to propositions in matters of religion. Throughout, he demonstrates his deep reverence for classical reason, especially as this is exemplified in Aristotle's forms of the syllogism. But Newman is enough of a psychologist to know that our acceptance of propositions, though usually influenced by formal modes of reasoning, is rarely reducible to them. Instead, our assent to a given idea is the consequence of a long and complex process, involving reasoning to be sure, but also hunch, intuition, prejudice, life experience, the example of great people who have made such an assent and the counterexample of bad people who have failed to do so. Newman cites in this context the almost Jamesian adage that "a man convinced against his will is of the same opinion still." And he observes that "some people are loud in praise of views that they do not hold."[19] The upshot is that assent is never identical to formal inference, never directly and simply correlative to the quality of logical argumentation used to support it. Rather, it is the result of a process as much nonrational as rational, as much bodily as intellectual, as much affective as reflective. Thus, to use Newman's own example, we know that Great Britain is an island, not because we have a clinching, irrefutable logical argument for it, but because "we have been so taught in our childhood, and it is so in all the maps; we have never heard it contradicted or questioned, every book we have read invariably took it for granted; ... numberless facts rest on the truth of it."[20] In other words, a wide variety of probable arguments, each one tending in the same direction and offering mutual support, leads the mind to make the leap to assent, even in the absence of compelling evidence.

And so, except in the most banal cases of mathematical inference ($2+2=4$), does the human mind actually function. In one of his university sermons, Newman compares the activity of the

mind to the moves of a mountain climber clambering his way up a
cliffside:

> The mind ranges to and fro, and spreads out, and advances
> forward with a quickness which has become a proverb, and a
> subtlety and versatility which baffle investigation. It passes on
> from point to point, gaining one by some indication, another
> on a probability, then availing itself of an association, then
> falling back on some received law, next seizing on testimony,
> then committing itself to some popular impression, or some
> inward instinct, or some obscure memory.[21]

Drawing from this source and that, pulled in one direction then
another, thinking, reacting, reaching down and ranging wide, the
mind comes to truth, not through "clear and distinct ideas," but
through a kind of instinctual, only quasi-rational play.

Wittgenstein, Goethe, James, and Newman — all critics of the
reductionism, subjectivism, and hyperrationalism of modernity, and
all celebrators of the playful, embodied, patient, and irreducibly
complex working of the mind. These thinkers all realize that knowing is a bloody and muddy process — not simply a bland looking
at things from a pristine height. They tell us that we have to plow,
climb, will, act, decide, push our way to insight — like painters
learning their craft, or baseball players learning how to swing the
bat, or like young philosophy students moving into Plato's world.
They know that minds are incarnate and that bodies are ensouled
and that all of us come to knowledge in a community of fellow
searchers, players, and apprentices. It is with these figures — and
consciously against the Cartesians — that I take my stand in this
book. I don't think we come to the way of Jesus through the privacy
of our inner experience, but rather through a lively intersubjective
play; I don't think we embrace the way of Christ by knocking down
the monuments of the Christian tradition, but rather by walking
around and through them, looking at them with admiration and
critical attention; and I don't think we find salvation through an
isolation of mind from body, but rather through the movements
and passions of the body. Christianity is a way, and we learn it by

walking; it is a river, and we know it by swimming; it is a game, and we come to love it through playing.

Being a Saint

A few years ago, I made a retreat at the Benedictine monastery of St. John's in Collegeville, Minnesota. In the course of my visit, I had several conversations with the eminent historian and liturgist Godfrey Diekmann, a man who had played a large role in the liturgical movement of the 1930s and 1940s and who had been a *peritus* at Vatican II. Ninety-two years of age but still spry and brilliant in conversation, Godfrey regaled me with stories of his various adventures and battles. After listening to him for several hours, I said, "Godfrey, if you were young again and could mount the barricades, what would you fight for in the church today?" Bringing his cane down on my knee, he said, without a moment's hesitation, "deification!" Not the answer I was expecting, but nevertheless an intriguing one. Throughout his career, Diekmann had taught the Greek fathers — Origen, Gregory of Nyssa, Basil the Great — and it is safe to say that their central motif was *theiosis*, rendered in Latin as *deificatio*, becoming divine. What these theologians meant was that the entire purpose of the Christian life was to make us, not simply better people, ethically upright, but to make us divine, to conform us to a participation in the life of the Trinity. Being holy, burning with the fire of God's own life, is the point.

Soon after his conversion to Catholicism, the young Thomas Merton was walking down a New York city street with his friend Robert Lax, also a recent convert. In the course of their conversation, Lax said to Merton, "Tom, what do want to be?" A bit surprised and befuddled, Merton responded, "Well, I guess I want to be a good Catholic." Lax fired back: "No, that's not it. You should want to be a saint!"[22] Merton said that this strange answer changed his life: from that moment on, he knew that Christianity was not primarily a matter of getting his ideas straight but rather getting his life straight. Hans Urs von Balthasar said that the only true theologians are the saints — those who have *practiced* the life of Jesus.

Christianity — like baseball, painting, and philosophy — is a world, a form of life. And like those other worlds, it is first approached because it is perceived as beautiful. A youngster walks onto the baseball diamond because he finds the game splendid, and a young artist begins to draw because she finds the artistic universe enchanting. Once the beauty of Christianity has seized a devotee, she will long to submit herself to it, entering into its rhythms, its institutions, its history, its drama, its visions and activities. And then, having *practiced* it, having worked it into her soul and flesh, she will know it. The movement, in short, is from the beautiful (it is splendid!) to the good (I must play it!) to the true (it is right!). One of the mistakes that both liberals and conservatives make is to get this process precisely backward, arguing first about right and wrong. No kid will be drawn into the universe of baseball by hearing arguments over the infield-fly rule or disputes about the quality of umpiring in the National League. And none of us will be enchanted by the world of Christianity if all we hear are disputes about *Humanae vitae* and the infallibility of the pope.

Christianity is a captivating and intellectually satisfying game, but the point is to play it. It is a beautiful and truthful way, but the point is to walk it.

Chapter One

Walking the First Path: Finding the Center

It is no longer I who live;
it is Christ who lives in me.
— Gal. 2:20

No storm can shake my inmost calm
while to that rock I'm clinging.
— Quaker Hymn

All along the watchtower princes kept the view
while all the women came and went
barefoot servants too.
— Bob Dylan

"God so loved the world that he sent his only Son, that all those who believe in him might have life in his name" (John 3:16). In his passion to set right a disjointed universe, God broke open his own heart in love. The Father sent, not simply a representative, spokesman, or plenipotentiary, but his own Son into the dysfunction of the world so that he might gather that world into the bliss of the divine life. God's center — the love between the Father and the Son — is now offered as our center; God's heart breaks open so as to include even the worst and most hopeless among us. As we saw, in so many spiritual traditions, the emphasis is placed on the human quest for God, but this is reversed in Christianity. Christians do not believe that God is dumbly "out there," like a mountain waiting to be climbed by various religious searchers. On the contrary, God, like the hound of heaven in Francis Thompson's poem, comes relentlessly searching after us. Because of this questing and self-emptying divine love, we become friends of God, sharers in the communion of the Trinity. That is the essence of Christianity; everything else is commentary.

It might seem odd to speak of the arcane doctrine of the Trinity as we begin a discussion of this first spiritual path, but without the Trinity, the center of which we speak would not exist. Not only is God active and aggressive enough to track us down in love; God is also "flexible" enough to include us in his own being. The Father sent his Son in order to gather us into the Spirit, which is the love that binds them together — and it is in this central place that we are privileged to exist. Whenever Christians pray, they invoke the names of the Trinitarian persons, because they are praying, not so much outside of God as a petitioner, as, strangely enough, *inside* of God as a sharer in the divine communion.

A new center comes to us as a divine gift, and our first responsibility is to welcome it. Paul Tillich said that the core of Christian faith is "accepting the fact that we have been accepted" — nothing simpler and nothing more elusive.[1] The twentieth-century German Catholic theologian Karl Adam declared that we believers "start at the top." We don't stand at the bottom of the holy mountain wondering whether we can clamber our way to the summit, attaining the divine through our heroic efforts. On the contrary, through God's grace, we start on the mountaintop, as the beloved children of God, cherished and redeemed. We practice this truth in Jesus' great prayer — beginning, not with supplication and self-deprecation, but with the bold claiming of God as our Father.

Thomas Merton wrote that the principal problem in the spiritual life is the Promethean temptation.[2] The Greek hero Prometheus, we recall, climbed Mt. Olympus and successfully stole fire from the gods to the infinite benefit of the human race. But the gods were anything but pleased with this theft, for they wanted to

hoard the fire as a divine prerogative. Consequently, they cap-
tured Prometheus, chained him to a rock, and sent an eagle each
day to chew out his liver. At the foundation of this story is the
conviction that the divine and the human are enemies and rivals.
The gods have treasures that they don't want us to have and we,
therefore, have to wrest them away through heroic achievement.
And this, Merton implies, is the problem. Deep down many of us
Christians still believe that God is a rivalrous Lord who dispenses
favors grudgingly, only after a demonstration of virtue on our part.
But the Good News is that the Greek and Roman gods, those capri-
cious and self-absorbed deities, have been exposed as frauds. The
true God is not one who loves in a niggardly or calculating way,
but one who *is* nothing but love, not one who offers himself as a
reward, but one who gives himself away as a gift.

Indeed one could say that the sin of Adam and Eve is precisely
this Promethean grasping at what God intends to give freely. God
forbids the eating of the tree of the knowledge of good and evil,
not because he wants to keep something from them, but because
the best and sublimest things can never be seized, only received.
And isn't the serpent's suggestion along Promethean lines: "God
knows that when you eat of this tree you will be like God, knowing
good and evil" (Gen. 3:5), and, by implication, he will resent it.
When they believed that lie, our first parents fell into the illusion
and torture of sin, convincing themselves that God is distant, demanding, jealous. And when they believed that lie, they sullied the
image of God within them, that is to say, the capacity to receive
in joy God's gift of himself. In the confusion of sin, this receptive
capacity became cramped, wary, and highly defended.

In his inaugural speech in the Gospel of Mark, Jesus tells the
people that God's kingdom is among them, and then he calls them
to *metanoia*, to a radical change of mind, body, heart, and soul.
What he is saying is this: God's love is now available unconditionally and without restriction, but you must change your whole life
if you are to receive it.[3] God's passionate concern has appeared in
the flesh, and so you can no longer live in the cramped space of the
Promethean attitude, and you can no longer entertain the illusory

convictions of the Promethean mind. Furthermore, this love must be the sole focus of your life. Neither money, nor fame, nor power, nor political party, nor nation state, nor culture can compete with it. To say with the Nicene creed, "I believe in one God, the Father Almighty," is to perform a subversive act, for it challenges the claim to ultimacy of any other person or thing or institution.

Thus this is the first path of holiness: finding the center which is the divine love. The most elemental way of the saint is to realize, with St. Paul, "it is no longer I who live but it is Christ who lives in me" (Gal. 2:20), that the organizing and energizing principle of one's life has shifted from the fearful ego to the love of Jesus. To walk this path is to know the *unum necessarium*, the one necessary reality around which everything else clusters and in terms of which everything else becomes meaningful.

The familiar story of the conflict between Martha and Mary (Luke 10:38–42) has often been interpreted as an account of the play between the active and the contemplative life, Jesus signaling his preference for the latter over the former. But I don't think that reading gets to the heart of it. It is rather a narrative concerning the spiritual problem of the one and the many. Martha complains that her sister is not helping her with the numerous and time-consuming tasks of hospitality and tells Jesus to do something about it. The Lord responds, "Martha, Martha, you are worried and distracted by *many things;* there is need of only one thing. Mary has chosen the better part which will not be taken away from her" (Luke 10:41–42). Martha's problem is not that she is busy or that she is engaging in the "active" life; her problem is that she is uncentered. Her mind, quite obviously, is divided, drifting from this concern to that, from one anxiety to another; there are *many things* that preoccupy her. What Mary has chosen is not so much the contemplative life, but the focused life. She is anchored, rooted in the *unum necessarium*, as the Vulgate renders this passage. The implication seems to be that, were Mary to help with the many household tasks, she would not be "worried and distracted" by them, since she could relate them to the center, and that, were Martha to sit at the feet of Jesus, she would still squirm with impatience, since her spirit is divided. As is so often the case in the spiritual life, the issue is not what they're doing, but how they're doing it. Indeed, the surest sign that something is off in Martha's soul is that she even tells God what to do!

We find something very similar in the stories of demonic possession in the Gospels. Notice first how often the demons speak in the plural. In Mark's account of the possessed man in the Capernaum synagogue, the unfortunate individual shrieks, "What have you to do with us, Jesus of Nazareth? Have you come to destroy us?" (Mark 1:24). This is a single person, but he speaks in the voice of the many, for the demonic consciousness is split, riven, uncentered. What cures the man is precisely the firm and authoritative voice of Christ—the one taming the many. And the same motif emerges in the account of the Gerasene demoniac a few chapters later. When Jesus asks the tormented man his name, he replies, "My name is Legion; for we are many" (Mark 5:9) — or in another even more vivid rendering, "for there are hundreds of us." Again, the psyche of the sinner is like a tempest, all wind and confusion. But we see something else here: like Martha, the demoniac orders Jesus around: "Send us into the swine; let us enter them" (Mark 5:12). *The* great mark of the disciple is obedience, abiding by the divine command; and the great mark of the anti-disciple is trying to master God.

Kierkegaard said that to be an integral person is to desire *one thing.* The saint is someone whose entire life, in all of its multifacetedness, circles like a vortex around one center of gravity: the broken heart of the divine compassion.

Evelyn Waugh's *Brideshead Revisited*

The archetype of this divine center appears over and again in the scriptural, theological, and spiritual worlds of Christianity, much as a musical motif occurs — now muted, now emphasized — in a great symphony. It has been expressed imagistically, narratively, doctrinally, and liturgically throughout the Tradition. In this sec-

tion I shall analyze a particularly beautiful literary manifestation of
this truth.

The contemporary English novelist David Lodge was asked what
makes his novels specifically Catholic. His response: they are all in
different ways about God's relentless pursuit of his errant children.
This answer has always put me in mind of one of the greatest religious novels of the twentieth century, Evelyn Waugh's masterpiece,
Brideshead Revisited.[4] The second "book" of *Brideshead* bears the
title "A Twitch upon the Thread," and this image is derived from
one of Chesterton's *Fr. Brown* stories: "I caught him [the thief]
with an unseen hook and an invisible line which is long enough to
let him wander to the ends of the world and still to bring him back
with a twitch upon the thread." Waugh's novel is about the process
by which God calls his children back to the center — even those
who have drifted to the furthest edge. As such, it is a particularly
apt illustration of the first path of holiness.

The story opens as Captain Charles Ryder and his troop, in the
course of their training exercises in the English countryside, come
upon a stately manor house called "Brideshead." This chance encounter triggers in Charles a flood of memories, for that place had
for many years been at the center of his emotional life. The novel
unfolds as the account of Charles's reminiscences of the people that
moved through that house and of the events that swirled around
it. What becomes plain in the course of the tale is that the central
character is none of the human figures, but rather the mansion
itself: indomitable, alluring, haunting Brideshead. St. Paul told the
Corinthians that Christ is the head of his body the church and,
shifting the metaphor, that Jesus is the bridegroom and the church
the bride. Waugh combines these two Pauline images, making of
Brideshead itself (the head of the bride) a powerful figure of both
Christ and the church. The novel is, accordingly, the complex account of how people circle around Christ, now fascinated, now
repelled, sometimes in his embrace, sometimes in flight from him.
It is about the power of the center.

Charles first comes to Brideshead through his relationship with
Sebastian Flyte, the eccentric second son of Lord and Lady March-

main. Sebastian had taken Oxford University by storm, not because of his intelligence or his accomplishments, or even his aristocratic heritage, but because of his remarkable good looks. Charles recalls: "I knew Sebastian by sight long before I met him. That was unavoidable, for, from his first week, he was the most conspicuous man of his year by reason of his beauty, which was arresting."[5] One night, after a bout of drinking, Sebastian appeared outside of Charles's first floor rooms and vomited through the open window, insinuating himself in the most oddly direct way into Charles's life. The next morning, he filled Charles's rooms with flowers as a sign of his repentance and invited him to lunch. In the course of that afternoon of champagne, eggs, lobster, and idiosyncratic conversation, Charles fell under the spell of Sebastian and the two became inseparable.

One morning Sebastian invited his new friend to accompany him on a ride in the country, and, after a few stops for wine and strawberries in idyllic settings, they came to "a new and secret landscape" where, through the trees, "prone in the sunlight... shone the dome and columns of an old house." This is Charles's first glimpse of Brideshead, Sebastian's home. Following his friend's lead, Charles explored the intricate beauty of the place: the gardens and fountain, the great central hall, the fireplace of sculptured marble, the gilt mirrors, and, most remarkably, the chapel, a riot of baroque decoration.

But what particularly impressed him was how this sumptuous place seemed to depress his friend: "I'm sorry," said Sebastian after a time, "I'm afraid I wasn't very nice this afternoon. Brideshead has that effect on me."[6]

His initiation into the enigma of the manor continued the following summer, during the long vacation, when he attended to Sebastian, who was convalescing from a minor injury. Even more deeply enchanted by the beauty of the place, Charles exclaims, "I... believed myself very near heaven during those languid days at Brideshead," and "if it was mine I'd never live anywhere else." Moving from room to room, admiring the variety of architectural styles and decorative motifs, convinced by the overall "logic" of the design, Charles says, "It was an aesthetic education to live within those walls." So intense was his artistic experience in the presence of the fountain at Brideshead that he could say, "I felt a whole new system of nerves alive within me, as though the water that spurted and bubbled among its stones was indeed a life-giving spring."[7] And the aesthetic delight was not restricted to the architectural and pictorial. One day Charles and Sebastian made their way to the cellars and discovered a cache of fine aged wines and, with the help of a book on wine-tasting, commenced to sample bottle after bottle. But the beautiful experience reached its high-point when Charles hit upon the idea of decorating the "office," a small room that opened on to the colonnade. As he painted delicate romantic scenes on the walls of that room, Charles realized his own artistic gifts, sharpening the technique and developing the style that would sustain him in his career as a professional painter.

The most obvious motif here is that of beauty as a route of access to the sacred. In the *Symposium*, Plato places in the mouth of Socrates the argument that a particular beautiful thing or person arrests the mind and then opens it to ever broader horizons of beauty, so that one is led from the love for a body to the love of the soul and then to love for glorious institutions and for the sciences and the forms and finally to the "open sea" of the Beautiful itself.[8] There is something similar in Dante's *Vita Nuova* and James Joyce's *Portrait of the Artist as a Young Man*. In both these works a man sees a strikingly alluring woman and is then inspired to dedicate his life to the pursuit and expression of beauty. Indeed, in Joyce's account, in a lovely evocation of the *Symposium*, the woman in question gazes out to sea.[9] Contemporary Catholic thinker Hans Urs von Balthasar bases his entire theological project on this intuition, constructing a "theological aesthetics."[10] For Balthasar, any beautiful object "chooses and calls" those who perceive it, summoning them to become missionaries on its behalf and ultimately compelling them to seek out the ground and source of beauty which is God.

In Waugh's narrative, Sebastian, with his "arresting" beauty (how Platonic), functions as the catalyst for Charles's quest. He falls in love with his friend, galvanized by the particularity of his physical attractiveness, and then is introduced, through him, to the more spacious confines of Brideshead's beauty, that is to say, the splendor of Christ's body. And like Dante and Joyce, Charles becomes himself a celebrator of the beauty that drew him, adding to the attractiveness of Brideshead through his own artistic contribution. Through one of its many charming ambassadors, the Beauty of the divine center has drawn someone to itself.

This interpretation is given added weight as we listen to the first explicit conversation that Charles and Sebastian have concerning the nature of Sebastian's Catholicism. Sitting with his friend on the veranda at Brideshead just after Sunday Mass, Sebastian suddenly announces: "O dear, it's very difficult being a Catholic." Surprised, Charles inquires, "Does it make much difference to you?" Comes the reply: "Of course. All the time." Influenced by the rationalism of his age and especially by the psychological theories that explain Christianity away as "the province of complexes and inhibitions," Charles pursues the issue with puzzled insistence: "But my dear Sebastian, you can't seriously *believe* it all... I mean about Christmas and the star and the three kings and the ox and the ass." Sebastian replies, "Oh, yes, I believe that. It's a lovely idea." Unaccustomed to such an aesthetic apologetic, Charles says, "But you can't *believe* things because they're a lovely idea." Undeterred, Sebastian counters, "But I *do*. That's how I believe."[11] In medieval philosophy, the good, the true, and the beautiful are identified as the transcendental properties of being. This means that whatever is, is desirable (good), knowable (true), and alluring (beautiful), and it furthermore implies that the three characteristics are mutually implicative. But from this it follows that any one transcendental property is a sign of the other two and that therefore, on strictly philosophical grounds, Sebastian is right in correlating belief to enchantment, truth to beauty: "That's how I believe."

And it is precisely in regard to this correlation that we can begin to understand the anomaly of Sebastian's discomfort at Brideshead. The center is not only alluring; it is also demanding, for it has, not only the soft edge of beauty, but the hard edge of truth. We saw that while Charles, from the first moment he saw it, exults in the glory of the place, Sebastian seems ill at ease, eager to be elsewhere. And this discomfiture of Sebastian's only deepens as the novel progresses, becoming the central dramatic knot of the first half of the story. Charles is in the first flush of his encounter with the enchanting quality of the center, whereas Sebastian has lived a lifetime with it and accordingly appreciates, painfully enough, what it entails. For the Beauty of God is not meant merely to entrance us; it is also designed to remake us according to its own image, so that we become that which we love.

The "demand" or truth of Brideshead is embodied in the intriguing character of Lady Marchmain, Sebastian's mother. Beautiful, cultivated, poised, Lady Marchmain reflects the elegance of the manor over which she presides. But she is much more than charming; she is also a fiercely devout and ethically upright Catholic who desires for her children moral as well as aesthetic excellence. From the very beginning of the novel, we sense Sebastian's fascination for and detestation of his mother. Though he admires and respects her, he seems in her presence to be permanently in an adolescent pout, and when she presses to make him a more responsible person, he responds with violent words and, eventually, withdrawal into alcoholism. Yes, Catholic faith is beautiful (indeed that is why Sebastian believes), but "Oh, how difficult it is to be a Catholic."

Sebastian's retreat from Brideshead and from his mother, we learn, echoes the earlier withdrawal of his father, Lord Marchmain. During the First World War, Lord Marchmain had left home and taken up with a mistress, finally settling in Venice, where he cultivated an elegant lifestyle and an exquisite hatred for his wife. During one of their vacations from Oxford, Charles and Sebastian visit Lord Marchmain and his mistress, Cara. While Sebastian and his father are away, Charles falls into conversation with Cara, who proceeds to spell out, with devastating honesty, the quality and texture of Lord Marchmain's feeling toward his wife. "He hates her; but you can have no conception how he hates her. . . . My friend, he is a volcano of hate. He cannot breathe the same air as she. He will not set foot in England because it is her home; he can scarcely be happy with Sebastian because he is her son. But Sebastian hates her too."[12] In the symbolism of Waugh's novel, father and son are both in violent and irrational rebellion against Christ, hating him because of what conformity to him would demand.

And these two rebels are joined by a third. As the terrible story of Sebastian's drunkenness progresses, we see Charles torn between loyalty to his friend and sympathy with Lady Marchmain. Again and again, she tried — through officials and dons at Oxford, through her other family members, by her own vigilance, and, most importantly, through Charles — to lure her son away from the dissolute life that he has embraced. But her efforts are in vain. On one particularly distressful Christmas visit, Lady Marchmain managed to block all of Sebastian's attempts to acquire alcohol, but she was ultimately tripped up by her son's best friend. Before he heads out for the hunt, Sebastian talks Charles into giving him some money so he can sneak off to a pub. When he returns hours later, obviously drunk, Lady Marchmain suspects how he had thwarted her. Calling Charles to her the next morning she asks, "Did you give Sebastian money yesterday . . . knowing how he was likely to spend it?" When he did not deny it, she said, "I don't understand it. I simply don't understand how anyone can be so callously wicked. . . . Did you hate us all the time? I don't understand how we deserved it?" Faced with the moral demand of the center, Charles had failed, and now he too felt obliged to go into exile from Brideshead, joining Sebastian psychologically as well as physically. But as he pulled away from the house, he knew that he was losing something precious and essential to his life: "As I drove away . . . I felt that I was leaving part of myself behind, and that wherever I went afterwards I should feel the lack of it, and search for it hopelessly, as ghosts are said to do."[13] The center had drawn him through its beauty, had charmed and entranced him, but then, when it demanded that his life become beautiful, he, like Sebastian and Lord Marchmain, balked and ran. But even from a distance, even while professing indifference, he would remain, despite himself, attached, haunted, or in terms of Chesterton's image, "hooked." And in time, the center would pull all of them back.

The final section of Waugh's novel is the account of the "twitch upon the thread" by which this divine pulling-back is effected. *Prima facie*, the story of Sebastian's decline, which is told intermittently in this section, is an unmitigated tragedy. Having eschewed his family and rejected their attempts to cure him of his alcoholism, Sebastian flees to Morocco, where he falls in with a thoroughly disreputable German named Kurt, who had shot himself in the foot in order to escape military duty and who is now hobbled by his suppurating wound. Supporting his pathetic friend both emotionally and financially and continuing his slide into desperate alcohol addiction, Sebastian seems a burnt-out case when Charles comes to visit him: this one-time English lord and Oxford dandy now an utter failure. But there is a sign of hope. When Charles wonders why in the world Sebastian wants to spend time with the hapless Kurt, Sebastian responds, "You know, Charles, it's rather a pleasant change when all your life you've had people looking after you, to have someone to look after yourself."[14] There we see it: the moral truth that corresponds to the beauty of Brideshead, the form of life that Sebastian had fled year after year, while clinging to the illusions of childhood. The beautiful life consists in love, the ecstatic act by which we leap out of ourselves in service of another. "The Son of Man has come, not to be served, but to serve and to give his life as a ransom for the many" (Mark 10:45). It is the attractiveness of this hard-edged truth that Sebastian is beginning to appreciate.

And it is the truth of love that continues to lure him even as his alcoholism progresses. Sebastian's youngest sister Cordelia — the child most like Lady Marchmain in attitude — tells the rest of his story in a dialogue with Charles. She had visited her exiled brother in Tunis and found him living with monks. Kurt had wandered away, and Sebastian had gravitated toward a monastery, where he had petitioned to be admitted as a lay brother and a missionary to the poorest of the poor. When this proved unfeasible because of his drinking, he simply insinuated himself in the world of the monks, becoming a sort of informal porter. When Cordelia saw him, he was in the infirmary, having collapsed after a particularly bad bout of drinking. She tells Charles: "They'd given him a room to himself; it was barely more than a monk's cell with a bed and a crucifix and white walls." Despite his many and obvious failings, despite the pitiful quality of his once promising life, Sebastian had become a favorite of the monks and had, in effect, become one of them. Clinging to the only hope that his secular imagination could conceive, Charles says, "It's not what one would have foretold; I suppose he doesn't suffer?" Cordelia responds from the standpoint of the Christian imagination, "Oh, yes, I think he does. . . . No one is ever holy without suffering."[15] Holiness involves suffering be-cause holiness finally is reduced to love, the forgetting of self. At the end of his journeyings, having wandered the earth to escape from Brideshead, Sebastian had, in effect, returned to it, finding joy in suffering love. "A twitch upon the thread."

An even more remarkable story of an exile returning is that of Lord Marchmain. Terminally ill and freed by the death of his hated wife, Lord Marchmain returns to Brideshead to die. Setting himself up in a great bed in one of the decorative rooms on the main floor and surrounded by the remaining members of his family, the old man waits in fear. As the days and months pass, he grows weaker both physically and psychologically. A priest is brought in to anoint him, but he brusquely dismisses him: "I am not *in extremis,* and I have not been a practising member of your Church for twenty-five years. . . . Show Father Mackay the way out."

When some weeks later Lord Marchmain slips into a semi-coma, the family gathers to discuss whether to invite the priest back, Charles and the doctor taking the negative position and the others the affirmative. After some emotional exchanges, the latter contin-gent wins out and Fr. Mackay is escorted into the sick-room. There the old man lies prone and nearly motionless. The priest bends over and blesses him saying, "I know you are sorry for all the sins of your life, aren't you? Make a sign if you can." Though there is no in-dication that Lord Marchmain has even heard him, Fr. Mackay continues with the rite of anointing, as the family members kneel around the bed. At this point, the agnostic Charles, Sebastian's fellow rebel, feels moved to pray, "O God, if there is a God, for-

give him his sins, if there is such a thing as sin." Suddenly, the old
man stirred. His right hand slowly made its way up to his forehead,
prompting Charles to fear that he would wipe the oil of anointing
away. But instead, "the hand moved slowly down his breast, then
to his shoulder, and Lord Marchmain made the sign of the cross."[16]
Against all expectations and despite a quarter-century of animos-
ity, the Lord of Brideshead comes home, marking himself, like his
son Sebastian, with the symbol of suffering love.

But these two returns are but preparations for the third and
greatest: that of Charles himself. He had, of course, never lost sight
of the center, since Brideshead had always remained an enchanted
place for him. But he had joined Sebastian *contra mundum* when
Lady Marchmain's pressure had been most intense. Then, through
many years of sadness he drifted — his marriage shipwrecked, his
career unsatisfying, his heart restless. However, a gradual alchemy
seemed to have been working in his soul all this time — perhaps
the effect of the prayers of many he had known at Brideshead —
and it reached a critical intensity when he heard the story of Sebastian's salvation and witnessed the penitence of Lord Marchmain.
That spontaneous prayer at the old man's deathbed was the most
vivid sign. In the novel's epilogue, set some time after the death
of Lord Marchmain, we rejoin the beginning of the book when
Charles and his troop came upon Brideshead. He makes his way
through the familiar corridors and comes at last to the chapel to
which Sebastian had introduced him long before. He notices the
tiny flame burning before the tabernacle signaling the presence of
Christ, and then he kneels and recites "a prayer, an ancient, newly
learned form of words."[17]

He was lured by its beauty, repelled by its demands and finally,
like Sebastian and Lord Marchmain, brought back by a twitch upon
the thread: the irresistible power of the center. The overarching
theme of Waugh's great novel seems to be that once one has been
entranced by Christ, there is, finally, no escape. To allow ourselves
to be found, accepting the fact that we are accepted, is to walk the
first path of holiness.

The Place of Safety and Power

Jesus blithely tells his disciples, "Do not fear those who kill the body but cannot kill the soul" (Matt. 10:28). In those words, a new world opens up. This command has nothing to do with the dualism of Greek philosophy whereby one is encouraged to eschew the goods of the body in order to release the soul. Jews simply didn't think that way. When Jesus speaks of "killing the body," he means the elimination of the entire person, the destruction of mind, muscle, imagination, and action, the total loss of self. And he says that we shouldn't worry about those who can do *only that!* What Jesus implies is that he has opened for his followers a new depth of existence, a new center, that cannot be touched even when the whole of what we customarily call the "self" has been destroyed. Through the power of his being, he has linked us to the creative source of all existence, the divine love which transcends the evanescence of space and time. And in that "place," loved in the Spirit by the Father and the Son, we are safe — even from those who would kill the body.

But this means that our perspective can and must change (*metanoia*). Most of us spend most of our lives defending ourselves against assaults on the "body," keen, almost every waking moment, to protect our psyches, our emotions, our fortunes, our health, our reputations. But Jesus is telling us that we shouldn't orient our lives that way ("Don't be afraid of those who can only attack those trivial goods"). When we do that, we warp ourselves, turning our lives defensively inward, living in a very small spiritual space. But when we live out of the divine center, we breathe the air of real spiritual freedom. No longer cramped fearfully around the "body," we can move into the wide expanse of the divine will, following God however he prompts us. And this state of affairs, this great soul, is, like Brideshead, simultaneously alluring in its beauty and terrifying in its demand.

In his commentary on Genesis, Origen offers a consistently Christological interpretation of the creation account.[18] The Bible tells us that, from the beginning of time, God's Spirit hovers over the face of the chaotic waters. For Origen, this brooding presence signals the divine mastery over that which is opposed to God's intentions, God's capacity to draw order from disorder, his greater "yes" to every possible "no." Those same waters appear, on Origen's reading, throughout the Scriptures: as the waters of the flood, as the tumultuous Red Sea, as the abode of Behemoth and Leviathan, as the stormy Sea of Galilee. In each case, the creative power of God masters the chaos and manages to draw order from it. Origen's primeval sea is thus like *das Nichtige* in the writings of Karl Barth, the "nothing" that resists the press and pull of God but which finally is powerless against it.

Now what is the specific agency by which God exerts his authority over the nothing? Interpreting, as was his wont, the Old and New Testaments together, Origen sees that it is the divine Logos: "In the beginning was the Word. . . . All things came into being through him, and without him not one thing came into being" (John 1:1–3). Whenever the creator God breaks the power of chaos, it is through his Word, that which, Isaiah tells us, never goes forth from God without working its effect. But we Christians know that this Word has been fully manifested and made visible in Christ Jesus: "the Word was made flesh and lived among us" (John 1:14). Therefore, Jesus is the hermeneutical key to creation; it is in him that we see the divine order mastering the chaos. We notice this interpretive intuition in Origen's reading of the creation of dry land. Through God's Word, earth appears from out of the waters of chaos, and on the earth all forms of life appear: "plants yielding seed, and fruit trees of every kind that bear fruit with the seed in it . . . living creatures of every kind, cattle and creeping things and wild animals of the earth of every kind" (Gen. 1:11, 24). In Christ, the divine Word went into the heart of darkness, down into the depths of the chaos of sin, "obediently accepting even death, death on a cross" (Phil. 2:8), and then came forth, having transformed that darkness into light, that trackless chaos into order. In the Paschal Mystery, Jesus creates, from the disorder and nothingness of sin, *terra firma*, a land full of life and fecundity. Jesus, in short, is the *center*, shelter from the storm, a sure place to stand even as the chaos of sin crashes around us. When we are rooted in the concerns of the "body," we become disordered, but when we are rooted in Christ, the crucified Logos of God, we burst with life of limitless variety. In this Origenistic reading, creation is not simply a cosmological category, but a psychological and spiritual one as well. It is a way of talking about the God-centered spirit.

We find something similar in Teresa of Avila's description of the soul as an "interior castle."[19] For a sixteenth-century Spaniard, a castle would be a place of safety, a keep. And this is, for Teresa, the nature of the center: even when the worst storms of life swirl around us, there is, at the deepest ground of the spirit, shelter and peace in the indwelling Christ. St. Paul knew about this castle when he said, "I am convinced that neither death nor life, nor angels nor rulers, nor things present, nor things to come, nor powers, nor height, nor depth, nor anything else in all creation, will be able to separate us from the love of God in Christ Jesus our Lord" (Rom. 8:38–39). Paul had faced the powers of the world; he had stood in the presence of death, he had experienced both the heights and the depths, but he was sure that none of them could shake the center that he had found in the Lord Jesus. Now there is more than protection in the interior castle; there is also power, for a castle is not only a defensive stronghold, but also a headquarters from which raiding parties can sally forth and subdue the enemy. Thus, when the center of the soul is secure, when we have oriented ourselves to the Head of the Bride, our lives tend to fall into harmonious patterns, Christ, as it were, conquering whatever is opposed to him.

In the course of my pastoral ministry, I met a young man who came to me seeking advice on how to pray. I didn't know him at all, and he volunteered no information concerning his background or life experience. I simply encouraged him to pray every day and, through a few simple practices, to focus on Christ as the center of his life. A few months later, he returned and told me that he had followed my advice. And then he said, without hesitation, "I really have to stop having promiscuous sex." Again, I had known nothing of his struggle, and all I could say was, "Yes, I agree with that." When I asked him how he had come to this conclusion, he replied,

"The daily prayer just began to work on me." This is the "offen-sive" dimension of the center: when Christ comes to dominate our lives, he draws all of our energies — physical, psychological, sex-ual, emotional, intellectual — around him, pressing them into his service. My guess is that, before he began to pray in a focused way, that young man didn't even realize how out of step his sexual en-ergies were. But Christ, the King of the interior castle, drew them to order. The persistence of his prayer meant that he had found something of the beauty of the center, and the resolution to change implied that he had been summoned by its truth as well.

In one of his homilies, St. Augustine offers a rich interpretation of the story of Jesus calming the storm at sea. The disciples in the boat stand for the church (the barque of Peter) making its way through the voyage of life. The wind and waves represent all that threaten us on the journey: failure, sickness, anxiety, depression, the attacks of our enemies, the fear of death itself. And the sleeping Christ symbolizes the inactivity of the true center. We have all been offered the divine power as the governing element of the soul, but we have allowed it to "fall asleep." As a result, we live, as the disciples in the boat, in constant terror, threatened on every side. Now when, in their terror, the disciples rouse the slumbering Jesus, he immediately calms the tempest. For Augustine, the message is clear: if you want peace in your soul, "wake up the inner Christ!" In his letter to the Ephesians, St. Paul says, "To him who by the power at work within us is able to accomplish abundantly more than all we can ask or imagine, to him be glory in the church and in Christ Jesus" (Eph. 3:20–21). Paul implies that our lives would be utterly transformed if we accessed that power, if we surrendered to it, if we stopped resisting it.

A like motif emerges in the writings of Teresa's colleague John of the Cross. Relying on a mystical tradition stretching back to the Song of Songs, John says that the inner Christ, is like a hidden wine cellar (shades of *Brideshead*).[20] This metaphor focuses, not on strength and safety, but on intoxication. The divine source, opened up by Christ, is an inexhaustible font of delight and elevation of consciousness. When we drink fine wine, we are lifted up out of our everyday preoccupations and become playful, imaginative, a bit daring. In the same way, when we drink of the spirit of Christ, the divine liquor, our minds are lifted up out of their obsessive concern with "the body" and opened to a higher, more joyful, dimension of experience. This inner wine cellar is buried within the souls of believers, but, says John of the Cross, most of us have lost the key.

How alluring it all is, and how elusive. The power of sin (which we will explore in the next chapter) keeps us out of the interior castle, far from the inner wine cellar. And this is why there is, necessarily, something harsh, uncompromising, and demanding about Christianity. It compels a decision and forces an all-or-nothing choice: with Christ or against him.

The Place of Detachment

According to legend, St. Laurence, in the midst of his torture on a red-hot gridiron, said to his tormentors, "Turn me over; I think I'm done on this side." On his way to Rome and a martyr's death, St. Ignatius of Antioch wrote to his followers urging them to let him be devoured quickly by the animals in the arena: "May the beasts become my tomb and may their teeth grind me like wheat." As he walked up the scaffold just before his beheading, St. Thomas More stumbled. Turning to the man who was accompanying him, More said, "Please give me a hand now; as for my coming back down, let me shift for myself!" When Br. Bill Tomes of Chicago hears that a gang war has broken out, he puts on his colorful and distinctive habit, hurries to the site of the battle, and stands in the midst of the gunfire until it stops. What gives these people the courage to do what they do? How can they face the greatest dangers calmly, even with a sense of humor? Grounded in the center who is Jesus Christ, they are detached from even those things that strike most of us as indispensable, even from physical life itself. Centered, they are free.

This theme of detachment can be found everywhere in the spiritual tradition. The Greek Fathers spoke often of holiness as a sort of *apatheia*, not "apathy" in the pejorative sense, but a rising above the passions and attachments of the worldly mind. In the mystical writings of John of the Cross, detachment from all the appetites of body, mind, and soul in order to attain the divine is practically the governing idea.[21] And certainly in the *Spiritual Exercises* of Ignatius of Loyola, spiritual *indiferencia* (not caring whether I have a long life or a short life, whether I am sick or well, whether I am rich or poor) plays a central role.[22] Only the person who has attained such freedom, the capacity to move wherever the Spirit prompts, is ready for the mission of Christ.

Anthony de Mello defines an attachment as anything in this world — including life itself — that we convince ourselves we cannot live without.[23] The implication, of course, is that in Christ we *can* live without anything in this world, and to know that in our bones is to be detached, spiritually free. To live in the infinite power of God is to realize that we *need* nothing other, that we *crave* nothing more, that we *can let go* of everything else. De Mello's attachment is very close to Augustine's *concupiscentia*, or errant desire. For Augustine, all of us have been wired for God ("you have made us for yourself") and therefore we are satisfied with nothing less than God ("our hearts are restless until they rest in you").[24] To become focused on something less than God (anything created, including our own lives) is therefore to place ourselves in spiritual danger and desperately to frustrate the will. Perhaps the best way to translate these notions of attachment and concupiscence into our contemporary jargon is by using the word "addiction." When we attach our wills to something less than God, we automatically become addicted, and this is the case precisely because the lack of satisfaction that we necessarily experience leads to an obsessive return, a compulsive desire for more and more. If that amount of money didn't quell my deepest desire, I must need more money; if that sexual encounter didn't satisfy the longing of my heart, I must need another more thrilling one, etc., etc. The initial thrill — the "rush" — of money, sex, or power conduces to an obsession that finally takes away our freedom and our self-possession.

Jesus describes the overcoming of this addiction with the evocative word "blessed," *makarios* in Greek. In Luke's version of the beatitudes, we find a pithy presentation of what the view from the center is like. First we are told "how blessed [*makarios*] are you who are poor" (Luke 6:20). We notice that there is none of the softening offered by Matthew ("poor in spirit"), but a simple and straightforward statement of the blessedness of being poor. How do we interpret what seems prima facie to be a glorification of economic poverty? Let me propose the following reading: "How lucky you are if you are not addicted to material things." One of the classic substitutes for God is material wealth, the accumulating of "things." Like any drug, houses, cars, and property provide a "rush" when they first enter the system, but then in time, the thrill that they provide wears off, and more of the drug must be acquired. This rhythm continues inexorably and tragically until the addict is broken by it. Once, on a Sunday afternoon, a knock came to the door of the rectory where I was staying. When I answered, I found a man, neatly dressed in expensive clothes and exuding confidence and self-possession. We sat down to talk, and he said, "Father, I've realized all of my dreams." "Well, that's wonderful," I responded benignly. "There's only one problem," he continued, "I'm perfectly miserable." It turned out that his dreams had to do almost exclusively with the accumulation of homes and the maintenance of an impressive stock portfolio. His education, his friendships, his social and professional life circled around and served that addictive and finally insatiable desire. The result according to the predictable physics of the soul: the crash into the misery that had taken possession of him. How "unlucky" for him to be tied up in such a net — and how necessary that he find the detachment of the first path of holiness.

Luke's beatitudes continue with "how blessed are you who weep now" (Luke 6:21). Again, we are struck by the oddness of the claim: how fortunate you are if you display the outward sign of greatest anxiety and depression. Might we translate it as follows: "How lucky you are if you are not addicted to good feelings." We live in a culture that puts a premium on good feelings and attempts to deny or medicate depression. But *feeling happy* is just as much a false god as wealth or power. It is, in itself, only an emotional state, a fleeting and insubstantial psychological condition that cannot possibly satisfy the deepest yearning of the soul; yet it is sought with as much compulsive frenzy as any other drug. We feel the "rush" of pleasure and then, when the thrill fades, we try at all costs to reproduce it at a higher pitch. It is in this context that the addictive use of drugs, alcohol, and artificial stimulants, as well as the hedonistic pursuit of pleasure in sex and at the table are to be understood. The person who lives in the center, the place of detachment, escapes (fortunately enough) this trap.

Luke's Jesus continues: "Happy are you when people hate you, and when they exclude you, revile you, and defame you on account of the Son of Man" (Luke 6:22). What could be stranger than this seemingly masochistic dictum? Again, some light might be shed if we translate it in terms of our hermeneutic of detachment: "How lucky you are if you are not addicted to the approval of others." Status, attention, fame are among the most powerful and insinuating of the false gods who lure us. When I was a child, I reveled in the praise that my father offered me because of my school work. But in time the thrill of that esteem wore off and I sought greater approval — first from my high school teachers, then from my college professors, then from graduate school instructors, and finally from my doctoral director. Each time I heard a word of praise, I felt the rush of the drug, but it was never enough. My life had become an unceasing quest for applause; I was trapped in the familiar pattern, needing approval as desperately as my body needed food and water. Jesus told his disciples: "Woe to you when all speak well of you" (Luke 6:26), and Winston Churchill said, "Never trust a man who has no enemies." The one whom everyone loves is in spiritual distress, since the good-will of the crowd has undoubtedly become that person's idol. As so many of the saints — and Jesus himself — witness, the path of spiritual freedom brings one almost inevitably into conflict with those who are still in chains. Those who have placed themselves in the Christ-center rest secure even as the approval of the fickle crowd waxes and wanes.

The freedom and fullness of detachment is probably no better expressed than in John of the Cross's beautiful mantra: "To reach satisfaction in all, desire satisfaction in nothing; to come to the knowledge of all, desire the knowledge of nothing; to come to possess all, desire the possession of nothing; to arrive at being all, desire to be nothing."[25] This fourfold *nada* is not a negation but the deepest affirmation, since it is a "no" to a "no." Desiring to possess all, desiring to be all is the nonbeing of attachment, the misery of addiction; desiring to possess nothing, desiring to be nothing is, accordingly, freedom and being. It is finally to see the world as it is, and not through the distorting lens of cupidity and egotism. It is the view from the center.

Practices for Path One

As we tour our way through this thicket of images and symbols evocative of the center, we must not forget the overall purpose of this study: to show the way which is Christianity and to articulate the *practices* by which we walk it. We remember our anti-Cartesian stance and our insistence that Christianity has as much to do with the body as with the mind. What, therefore, are the practices that help us to stay on this first way? What precisely is the form of life that corresponds to finding the center?

Practices of Prayer

I am almost hesitant to speak of prayer because the usual descriptions of it have become so vague, abstract, and unchristian. But particular modes of prayer are indispensable practices of the first path, since they are conscious attempts to focus our lives on Christ the center. First, as we saw, when Christians pray, they are not addressing God from some external standpoint; they are not approaching the divine simply as a seeker or supplicant or penitent. They are *in* the divine life, speaking to the Father, through the Son and in the Holy Spirit. It has been said that Christian prayer is listening intently as the Father and the Son speak about you. It is this peculiar intimacy — praying in God and not just to him — that gives the Christian practice of prayer its unique texture.

Second, Christian prayer is an embodied business. In C. S. Lewis's *Screwtape Letters,* one of the recommendations that the training devil gives to his young charge is to encourage his "client" to think that prayer is something very "interior" and "mystical," having little to do with posture or the position of the body.[26] He wants the poor man to think that whether one stands, slouches, sits, or kneels is irrelevant to the quality of one's communication with God. This, of course, is the Cartesian voice, the dualist conceit. Behind Lewis's counterposition is a very Jamesian instinct. In the *Principles of Psychology,* James says that it is not so much sadness that makes us cry as crying that makes us feel sad, the body in a significant sense *preceding* the mind. So when we pray, it is not so much keen feelings of devotion that force us to our knees as kneeling that gives rise to keen feelings of devotion.

The centrality of gesture, posture, and movement in the act of prayer has long been taken for granted in the Christian tradition. Thus in the Hesychast movement in Eastern Christianity, great stress is placed upon the act of breathing while reciting the mantra-like "Jesus prayer." This is an adaptation of the words of the publican in Jesus' parable: "Lord Jesus Christ, Son of God, have mercy on me a sinner." While one prays the first part of the mantra, one is encouraged to breathe in deeply, filling the lungs entirely. This act symbolizes the filling of the heart with the living presence of Christ, the placing of Jesus at the center of all that we are. At the conclusion of this first part of the prayer, one holds one's breath for a brief period and then exhales while reciting the conclusion: "Have mercy on me a sinner." This last gesture evokes the expelling of sin from the heart. The double movement — breathing in and breathing out — is thus a sort of cleansing process, a taking in of the Holy Spirit and a letting-go of unclean spirits.

In certain monasteries of the Hesychast tradition, almost the whole of the monk's day is taken up with the recitation and practice of the Jesus prayer, sometimes formally and intentionally and other times informally and instinctually. The beauty of this prayer is that it can be practiced at any time of the day or night and in nearly any setting or circumstance. One can set aside an hour for intense and concentrated breathing-prayer or one can steal two minutes in the midst of a hectic day. Or the prayer (and the feel of it in one's lungs and body) can become second nature, automatic, a constant accompaniment of one's activity and inactivity. My grandmother used to pray the Jesus prayer in this way, breathing it out almost inaudibly whenever she sat down. However it is practiced, it is a vivid way of reminding the body of the center.

Another intensely bodily (though much maligned) practice of prayer is the rosary. Anthony de Mello said that simply the feel of rosary beads on his fingers often put him into a mystical frame of mind (how Jamesian!).[27] For me, the most striking quality of the rosary prayer is its deliberate pace, the way it, despite ourselves, slows us down. It is a commonplace of the spiritual masters that the soul likes to go slow. This is because it likes to savor. Thomas Aquinas said that there are two basic moves of the will — to seek after the good that is absent and to rest in the good possessed. We contemporary Westerners are particularly adept at the first exercise of the will and rather inept with regard to the second. We love to race to our next appointment, to get to our destination as fast as possible, to overcome all obstacles efficiently, but then we often find ourselves at a loss, restless, when we actually get where we wanted to go. Savoring eludes us. When we pray the rosary, we repeat a few simple prayers over and over, and we move in a circle, arriving at the very place we started. The purpose of the exercise is not to *get* particularly anywhere; rather it is to meditate upon the great mysteries of Christian salvation, to look at the "pictures" of Jesus' birth, suffering, death, resurrection, and ascension from a variety of angles, in varying moods, with different emphases, the way we might muse over a Rembrandt portrait.

Like the Jesus prayer, the rosary is a mantra, that is to say, a prayer of almost hypnotic repetition. Masters in the Buddhist tradition of meditation speak of "calming the monkey mind." This means the settling of the superficial mind which dances and darts from preoccupation to preoccupation and whose concerns tend to dominate our consciousness: "What is my next appointment? Where do I go next? What did she mean by that?" In order to open up the deepest ground of the soul — what we have been calling the center — that mind must be, at least for a time, quelled. In the rosary meditation, the mantra of the repeated Hail Marys quiets the monkey mind, compelling it to cede place to deeper reaches of the psyche.

When I was engaged in full-time parish ministry, I saw rosaries frequently — wrapped around the fingers of the dead at wakes. This association of the rosary and death is appropriate, since the Hail Mary is, among other things, a *memento mori*, a reminder of death. The prayer ends with the petition, "Holy Mary, Mother of God, pray for us sinners, now and at the hour of our death," and therefore when the entire meditation is practiced, one calls one's own death to mind fifty times. What a wonderful way of relativizing the myriad concerns of the ego and placing oneself in the presence of the deepest center! A decentering of the ego almost necessarily occurs when we program into our fingers, our voices, and our minds that we are going to die.

Finally, however we pray, as Christians we pray *for each other.* If the essence of prayer is resting in God's creative love, then whenever we pray, we are linked, willy-nilly, to everyone and everything else in the cosmos. In the divine still-point we find the ground from which all things proceed and by which they are sustained. And thus, the very act of prayer is, necessarily, communal and corporate. Charles Williams took as the elemental principle of the Christian life the play of co-inherence, that is to say, existing in and for the other.[28] Just as the Father gives himself away totally in the Son and the Son returns the favor by existing totally for the Father, so all creation is, at its best, marked by this metaphysics of co-implication, co-involvement. There is a hint of co-inherence in the radical interdependency of the things of nature, but it is more apparent in the complex and dramatic interpenetrations of human psyches, bodies, and souls. I am able, in love, to place my mind in your mind and to project my will into yours, in such a way as to bear your burdens. When Christians speak of praying for one another or, even more radically, of suffering on behalf of one another, they are assuming this ontology of co-inherence. Of course, its greatest archetype (after the Trinity itself) is the substitutionary sacrifice of Christ on the cross, whereby Jesus truly suffered *for* the world, his pain literally taking away the pain of a sinful world. This sort of language becomes coherent only in light of the unifying power of the center.

Pilgrimages and Processions

At the beginning of the *Canterbury Tales,* Chaucer evokes the beauty and *élan* of springtime — the sweet showers of April, the burgeoning of the plants, the singing of the birds — and then he tells us that this surge of life awakens in people a peculiar desire: "Thanne longen folk to goon on pilgrimages."[29] Springtime was the season when medieval Europeans left the security of home and set out on lengthy journeys — risking disease, robbery, even death — in order to look at the relics of saints or to stand in holy places. In the case of Chaucer's pilgrims, of course, the destination was the Cathedral of Canterbury and the grave of the "hooly blissful martyr" Thomas à Becket. But Christians moved all over Christendom on these journeys — to see the tomb of the Wise Men at the Cologne Cathedral, to visit the grave of St. James at Compostela, to commune with St. Mary Magdalene at Vezelay, to stand near the Holy Sepulchre in Jerusalem, to be with Peter and Paul in Rome. That last expression — "to be with" — probably best evokes the mentality of these pilgrims, for they were not, for the most part, simply tourists or souvenir hunters (though there was quite a trade in relics!); they were spiritual seekers who sincerely felt that they could establish a personal contact with saints at the site of their life and death.

On the floor of Chartres Cathedral in France is inscribed an extraordinary design, a labyrinth forty-two feet in diameter consisting of one path, twisting and folding intestine-like upon itself, and leading toward a circle at the center.[30] During the Middle Ages, a depiction of the heavenly Jerusalem rested in this circle, and it is believed that pilgrims to Chartres would follow the way of the labyrinth on their knees, moving deliberately from the circumference to the center. This winding and painful journey was intended as a compensation for those who, for whatever reason, couldn't make the actual pilgrimage to the Holy Land.

In the early twentieth century, the French mystic and writer Charles Péguy revived the custom of making a journey on foot to Chartres, and hundreds of young people continue in this tradition to the present day. In his novel *Therapy*, David Lodge tells the story of a man passing through a rather rocky midlife crisis. After trying every type of therapy available to late-twentieth-century civilization — psychotherapy, acupuncture, aromatherapy, sexual affairs — his character finally finds some semblance of peace in the reading of Kierkegaard and in undertaking, like his medieval forebears, the arduous pilgrimage to St. James of Compostela. As Carl Jung knew, the deepest psychological healing is always a spiritual healing. And isn't *Brideshead Revisited* a story of a particularly lengthy and dangerous but finally successful pilgrimage?

Why were (and are) these public displays of Christian faith so important? And what spiritual energy animates them? I think it has to do with movement. We have seen that Jesus' inaugural address concerns *metanoia*, the turning around of our lives, the act of going beyond the attitude and stance that we have. We must eschew the various false gods that we have been pursuing and find the true God; we must turn from the periphery of the soul and discover the depth of the soul. Accordingly, change of direction and movement are both vital to the Christian way. It is interesting to note how much movement there is in the Scriptures: Abraham going from Ur to the Promised Land; the children of Israel crossing the Red Sea from slavery to freedom; the Jews being carried off to Babylon and then coming home; Jesus setting his face to Jerusalem and going resolutely up to Zion. The Bible is full of pilgrimages. When the medieval pilgrim set out on a journey to a holy place, she was giving bodily expression to spiritual movement, acting out with her whole person the process of conversion. To travel to Compostela or Rome or Jerusalem — with all the attendant dangers and difficulties — was to mimic the arduousness of the spiritual path, and to arrive at those holy destinations was to act out the finding of the center.

Can this practice still be part of the Christian way? In recent

years, Manila, Paris, Compostela, Denver, and Rome have all been
pilgrimage sites for the youth of the Catholic world. So many young
people gathered in Mile High stadium in Denver that their cheers
literally buffeted the pope's helicopter as it came in for a landing;[31]
so great a crowd assembled in Paris that young people, joining
hands, were able entirely to circle the city; and World Youth Day
in Manila constituted the largest single gathering in human history. The attractiveness of the pilgrimage seems not to have faded.
And what is particularly powerful about these events is their *public*
nature. Modernity, as we have seen, can tolerate religion as long
as it is safely sequestered in the privacy of one's conscience or
practiced behind closed doors. What challenges modernity is a religion that shows up. A secularized culture wants us to believe that
processions and pilgrimages are somehow inappropriate, sectarian,
trouble-making. I think we should make a little trouble.

Why couldn't we encourage young people in this country to
make a pilgrimage to the National Shrine in Washington, or to
the tomb of Mother Cabrini in New York, or to Martin Luther
King's shrine in Atlanta, or to Guadalupe in Mexico City? Or why
couldn't we encourage groups to make a journey to one of our
great monasteries — St. Meinrad, Gethsemani, Snowmass? Or why
not just a candlelight march through a parish neighborhood, consciously claiming it for Christ, or a procession with relics, bringing
the saints to the community? And why not Corpus Christi processions outdoors, moving the Blessed Sacrament through the city
streets and May crownings preceded by songs and displays? These
are all embodied ways of centering our lives on Jesus Christ, all
profoundly nondualist means of walking the first path of holiness.

Medals, Crosses, and Garb

The Englishwoman Susan Howatch has written a series of novels
dealing with the Church of England in the twentieth century.[32]
The character who functions as the spiritual touchstone for all of
the books is Jonathan Darrow, mystic, monk, seer, and director of
souls. In times of crisis, Howatch's heroes and heroines, willingly
or not, usually find their way to Darrow for comfort and counsel.

Along with offering what we might call psychotherapy and spiritual direction, Darrow often makes a surprising recommendation. He urges troubled persons to carry a crucifix, especially when they might be confronting special temptation or anxiety. When this suggestion is met with resistance or skepticism, Darrow responds, "No demon can withstand the power of Christ." Now to his enlightened modern interlocutors (especially those influenced by the Low Church wing of Anglicanism), this seems like so much superstition: the carrying of talismans to ward off devils. But Darrow explains that the touching of the crucifix focuses the entire personality on the power of Christ — centering and grounding it — and that this act wards off all of those powers, interior and exterior, that seek to unravel the unity of the soul. What I have always appreciated in Darrow's approach is its profound anti-Cartesianism. He knows that spiritual integrity is effected, not simply by interior processes, but also by the moves of the body, Christ entering through touch as much as through thought or feeling.

Obviously Howatch's Darrow is drawing on an old and rich tradition within Christianity, one that has, unfortunately, fallen into desuetude in the last several decades. In our largely secularized culture, the carrying or wearing of religious symbols strikes even the believer as somewhat embarrassing, just not the done thing. But a crucifix or medal around one's neck or a religious pin worn on one's clothing can serve, not only as a public witness, but as a powerful centering device. In the course of the day, when beset by a dozen worries and distractions, a believer can simply touch that symbol and thereby effect that gathering of the soul that Darrow described.

In 1993, I attended the Parliament of the World's Religions, a meeting of representatives from, it seemed, every major and minor religious group on the planet. At one session, I sat down next to a bearded man swathed in robes from head to foot, carrying a kind of rosary in his hand and smiling benignly. I presumed he was a spiritual teacher from one of the Hindu traditions. During the question and answer period, he raised his hand, and I expected to hear him speak in the dulcet tones of India, but when the question came forth, it was in the not so dulcet tones of middle America. It turned out that he was a former Catholic priest from Cleveland! Now this assessment could be completely wide of the mark, but I would be willing to bet that when that man was a priest, he wouldn't have been caught dead either carrying a rosary or wearing religious garb. Over the past thirty years, Catholics have, as I have argued, abandoned many of their practices, and one of those was the donning of distinctive clothing to signal one's spiritual commitment. Priests, monks, and nuns rather aggressively secularized themselves, preferring to wear street clothes and tending to see religious habits as indicative of clericalism. But during this period, many Christians turned longingly to the Eastern spiritual traditions, finding there the very practices and forms of life that they missed in secularized Christianity. Somehow, it was a problem for their priest to wear a cassock or Roman collar, but it was perfectly fine for their Buddhist master to wear a distinctive habit.

Now I am not calling for some wholesale return to habits and collars, but I am arguing that "spiritual dress" is one of the practices that our Christian tradition has long reverenced. It is a way of signaling to the body and soul that there is something different and deeply challenging about the Christian style of life. Let me illustrate this through reference to a perhaps surprising source. In his autobiographical reflection *Confessions*, Matthew Fox recalled his year as a Dominican novice. "We rose about 5:00 A.M. in pitch darkness and made our way downstairs to the chapel, where we spent ninety minutes chanting the psalms, praying and attending mass. . . . We had chores to do — cleaning the building, the toilets, working in the yard, planting flowers. There were also occasions for outdoor sports — football, volleyball, baseball, hockey, hiking. But most of all we had time for reflection, reading, meditation." We notice here, of course, the process of initiation into a new world, an apprenticeship to a form of Christian life involving the body as much as the soul. But one of Fox's most vivid memories had to do with the donning of the garb of his order for the first time: "We took off our black suit coats and were frocked in a shiny new white Dominican habit that smelled of something so unique to itself that I have no words for it even today."[33] What a sensual, anti-Cartesian description! Fox remembers, not only the color and feel of the garment, but its aroma as well. In the early centuries of the church, the ritual of baptism included a similar change of clothes. Candidates stripped down (symbolizing the casting off of the old person), oiled up (chrismated, Christified), and then plunged into the water (dying and rising with Jesus). Finally, they were clothed in a white garment (not unlike the Dominican habit) evocative of the new risen life. When people were baptized in those days, they *knew*, in their minds and their bones, that they had *put on* the Lord Jesus both inside and out.

Is there a way for Christians to recover this traditional practice? Obviously, religious could become a bit less reticent about their distinctive habits, seeing them, not as expressions of superiority, but as a witness to a culture grown forgetful of the spiritual dimension. And lay Christians could cultivate the practice of wearing a cross, a crucifix, or a ring — some mark of their faith — when they move about in the world. Or they could don a particular garment, an alb or a scapular, when they pray. In these small ways, Christians could remind themselves (and others) of the center which grounds and transcends all of the concerns of the secular.

Fr. Benedict Groeschel heads a community of Franciscan friars in the Bronx who work with the homeless and poor. One of their distinctive marks is the wearing of a full, grey Franciscan habit, replete with scapular, knotted cincture, and a lengthy hood. Their hope, in part, is to provoke surprise: "Who are these holdovers from the Middle Ages moving about in the modern world?" When one of his novices balks, embarrassed to wear this hard-to-miss garb in the middle of secularized New York, Groeschel responds, "Actually, there is no better place to wear a habit than in New York, where you see every kind of exotic outfit. If someone stares at you, just look back and say, 'You must be from out of town!' " There has been a bit too much embarrassment on the part of believers, too much of a desire not to be stared at. Maybe it is time for us to raise a few eyebrows.

Fasting

We saw that one of the signs of living in the center is detachment, the calming of concupiscent desire. When we are rooted in Christ Jesus, we are no longer dominated by the lust for the false gods of power, privilege, wealth, and prominence. But that freedom — that acceptance of being accepted — is not a matter of course; rather, it is acquired through an array of spiritual practices and disciplines which shape desire.

A most important one is fasting. The television stations seem to have a never-ending supply of footage of overweight people lumbering around. Whenever they run a report on the increasing problem of obesity in America, they trot out these tapes and we see ourselves: bloated and overfed. It is clear that obesity is a complex issue, involving both physical and psychological components, but, if our tradition is right, it is also a spiritual issue, since it indicates a form of concupiscence, errant desire. The appetites for food and drink are so pressing, so elemental, that, unless they are quelled and disciplined, they will simply take over the soul. They are like children who clamor constantly for attention and who, if indulged, will in short order run the house. Therefore, if the desire for the center, the passion for God, be awakened, the more immediately pressing desires must be muted, and this is the purpose of fasting in its various forms. We force ourselves to go hungry so that the deepest hunger might be felt and fed; we force ourselves to go thirsty so that the profoundest thirst might be sensed and quenched. In a way, fasting is like the "calming of the monkey mind" effected by the rosary prayer: both are means of stilling the effervescence of relatively superficial preoccupations.

But food and drink are not the only objects of concupiscent desire. We saw that material things and wealth are also ready substitutes for the center. Thus, a kind of fasting from money and what it can buy is an important practice of the Christian community. How often in the Gospels Jesus recommends that his disciples "sell all they have" or "abandon everything" or "give to the poor," and how often throughout the Christian tradition has the discipline of almsgiving been emphasized. In the Acts of the Apostles, we hear that the earliest community of believers sold their belongings and laid the proceeds at the feet of the apostles for equitable distribution (Acts 4:35).

So how does a community behave who find their security, not in wealth, but in Jesus Christ? They could embrace the ancient biblical practice of tithing, giving 10 percent of their income to the poor or to the church. They could place in their homes, right by the door, an alms box, and each time they leave, they could put something in it for those who have little. They could set an extra place at their family table and they could give what they would have spent on that meal to the brother or sister who does not have enough to eat. They could go into their probably overstuffed closets on a regular basis and take out shirts, pants, and dresses for those who need them. (St. Ambrose said that if the Christian has two shirts in his closet, one belongs to him; the other belongs to the man with no shirt. And Pope Leo XIII, in his social encyclical *Rerum Novarum* stated that, once the demands of necessity and propriety are met, everything that a person owns should be directed to the common good.)[34] Or they could find the car, stereo, home, or television that they want and could afford and then purposely buy a less expensive model, giving the difference to the poor. Or, realizing that concern for the homeless and the hungry in their community is not an abstract "social problem," but rather the concrete responsibility of Christians, they could directly spend their wealth to feed and house those in need.

For years, one of the best-known practices in the Catholic tradition was the Friday abstinence from meat. By this modest act of self-denial, Catholics identified themselves with the sufferings of Christ on Good Friday, signaling with their bodily behavior a focus upon the center. But another advantage of this practice — often overlooked — was the social bond and corporate sensibility that it created among Catholics; it was a public act that identified them as a unique social group, establishing a clear line of demarcation between themselves and others. Now there is no question that the importance of this gesture became, in some cases, exaggerated (eat meat on Friday and go directly to hell), and it was, accordingly, muted in the period after Vatican II, becoming, first, a voluntary, self-imposed discipline and then passing largely into oblivion. Both anthropologist Mary Douglas and historian Eamon Duffy have commented on the deleterious effects of this suppression. Duffy recalls that when the English bishops relativized the fasting obligation in the late 1960s, a dramatic interiorization and individualization of Catholicism followed. The moment we say that a shared practice is "up to the individual," the social bond that it formerly produced is lost. And Douglas has similarly demonstrated that the privatization of fasting requirements undermined a whole complex of ritual and symbolic connections by which corporate identity was preserved.[35] What both these commentators saw in the suspension of abstinence laws was the modernizing, the Cartesianizing, of Catholicism. And in this the capacity of the Catholic community to define itself and to speak a challenging word to the culture — even in a simple way — was seriously compromised.

We recall that another of the Lukan Jesus' puzzling beatitudes was "blessed are you who weep," that is to say, lucky are you who are not addicted to the false god of good feelings. Now as an ardent Chestertonian, I certainly subscribe to the dictum "wherever the Catholic sun doth shine / there is music and laughter and good red wine" and stand, accordingly, against puritanism in all its forms. There is nothing life-denying or teetotaling or pleasure-eschewing about authentic Christianity; it embraces the joys of human existence with great enthusiasm. However, let me make at least a nod in the direction of the Puritans. Since pleasure — like all good created things — can become an attachment, it too must be disciplined if we are to stay rooted in the center. To stand with Christ is hardly to embrace a hedonistic campaign of marching from delight to delight; rather it is to do the will of the Father even when that costs dearly, even when it conduces to the cross. Therefore the centered person must be ready for pain as well as pleasure, for deep sadness as well as contentment, clinging neither to one nor to the other. (We recall how Brideshead sometimes delighted Charles and other times disgusted him; and we remember how Sebastian fled miserably from Brideshead into a life of pain-avoidance.)

And therefore the practice of limiting (and in some cases eliminating) our intake of artificial stimulants and mood-enhancers is a solidly Christian one. Addiction to alcohol, various types of drugs, and, in more recent years, antidepressants such as Prozac is part of a journey away from the center. Several commentators have weighed in with the view that artificially induced "good feeling" is lessening some persons' contact with the density and complexity of a full human life, severing them, in fact, from the sources of deep happiness. From a Christian standpoint, the relentless pursuit of pleasure (or, what often amounts to the same thing, the flight from pain) undermines the mission, since the mission is tied to neither pleasure nor pain. So we Christians don't have to put up a false front — smiling at all comers and laughing at every joke. We know that it is permissible, even blessed, to weep.

And so we resist Screwtape's suggestion that we spiritualize our faith. And we find the center with the whole self — praying, breathing, fingering beads, walking, processing, pilgrimaging, and fasting our way along the first path of holiness.

Chapter Two

Walking the Second Path: Knowing You're a Sinner

We're all in the same boat; and we're all seasick.
—G. K. CHESTERTON

God is in his heaven
and we all want what's his
but power and greed and corruptible seed
seem to be all that there is.
—BOB DYLAN

Go away from me, Lord, I'm a sinful man.
—Luke 5:8

G. K. Chesterton once said, "There are saints indeed in my religion: but a saint only means a man who really knows that he is a sinner."[1] As far as Chesterton is concerned, the relevant distinction is not between sinners and nonsinners, but rather between sinners who know it and those who don't. But this clarification is of tremendous moment, for sin is known only through contrast with grace, just as shadow is appreciated only in contradistinction to light. And thus people who can acknowledge their sins are, at least to some degree, participating in the center; they are, in a word, saints.

Chesterton's principle is confirmed by the peculiar fact that it is precisely the great saints who seem most acutely aware of their imperfections. When Isaiah saw the magnificent display of God's glory in the temple, he said, "I am a man of unclean lips!" (Isa. 6:5). And when Peter witnessed the miraculous draught of fishes, he fell at the feet of Jesus and said, "Go away from me, Lord, for I am a sinful man" (Luke 5:8). Even Thérèse of Lisieux, the beloved and innocent "Little Flower," claimed that she was the worst of sinners. When we hear such protestations from the holiest of people, we are tempted to write them off as so much false modesty, but this would be a serious spiritual mistake.

In Chicago during the wintertime tons of salt are dumped on the roadways to keep them clear of ice and snow, but then that salt is kicked up onto cars and windshields. When one is driving at night, away from direct lighting, one can see fairly well, even through a salt-caked windshield. But come the next morning, when one is driving straight toward the rising sun, that same windshield is suddenly opaque. John of the Cross said that the soul is like a pane of glass and God's love is like the sun.[2] It is, accordingly, when God's love is shining most directly on the soul that its smudges and imperfections are most apparent. We sinners spend our time riding away from the divine light, our lives focused on money, sex, power, and our own egos; and thus it is not the least bit surprising that we remain relatively unaware of our sinfulness. But the saints, the ones who have directed their lives toward the light and heat of God, are most cognizant of all that still remains incomplete in their souls. Saul of Tarsus galloped off to Damascus to persecute the church of Christ, utterly convinced that he was following the will of God. And then he was struck blind by the light of God's presence (Acts 9:3). When the true God appeared to him, he, suddenly and salvifically, did not know where he was going. In Caravaggio's painting of this scene, Saul is a young man, well-muscled and lean, and he is clothed in the raiment of a soldier. Everything in his body and his array suggests focus, energy, and aggressive confidence. But in the wake of the shock of the light, he lies on the ground, eyes shut, arms groping into the darkness, his confidence dissipated. And it is at this moment that he begins to be a saint.

In recent years there has been a reticence among Christians to speak frankly of sin and divine judgment. When I was coming of age in the Catholic Church — in the late sixties and seventies — we passed quickly over the themes of sin and God's anger, convincing ourselves that they were obsolete Old Testament ideas trumped by the compassion and forgiveness of the New Testament, or that they contributed to low self-esteem. In point of fact, the New Testament is replete with references to sin and to the threat of eternal damnation (most often on the lips of Jesus himself). And, as we have seen, a frank acknowledgment of one's dysfunction is not a signal of psychological debility; just the contrary, it is an indication that one has finally directed one's life toward the light. It is not the neurotics but the saints who can say they are sinners.

Much of this paradox is caught in the happily double sense of the Latin word *confessio*. This term can mean, as in the English translation "confession," an acknowledgment of wrongdoing, but it also has the sense of "profession" or even "proclamation." Thus the church speaks, in this second sense, of its "Confessors," those great spokespersons for the truth of Christianity. We can confess, in the first meaning of the term, in the measure that we have first confessed in accord with the second meaning. Only when we stand in the center, bathed in the light of Christ, can we notice what remains dark in us. It is, of course, that master of the Latin language St. Augustine who so carefully entitled his spiritual testament *Confessiones*. In that text we find ample evidence of the confession of sins (in fact the pages practically drip with his tears of repentance), but that confession is made possible by the even more primordial profession of praise that rings out from every passage.

And this is why one of the practices of the Christian way is a stark confrontation with the reality of sin. When we enter a Gothic cathedral, we are plunged into darkness, as our eyes strain to adjust from the brightness outside to the somberness of the church interior. This is not accidental. The architects of the cathedrals wanted to remind us, as we enter into the realm of the holy, that we are a people who walk in darkness.[3] They knew that it was simply inappropriate for anyone to stride confidently into the divine presence, and it was thus that they threw us purposely off balance.

One of the principal themes in the writing of Flannery O'Connor is precisely this awakening to sin and, consequently, to the need for salvation. It is no more evocatively expressed than in a short story she wrote toward the end of her life entitled "Revelation." The tale commences with the entry of Mr. and Mrs. Turpin into the tiny and packed waiting room of a doctor's office.[4] The room is filled with sick people, but the plump and well-dressed Mrs. Turpin is decidedly not one of them: she is quick to tell everyone that her husband is the one who needs to see the doctor. As the story progresses, we hear two conversations: the outer one that Mrs. Turpin has with everyone in the waiting room and the inner one that she carries on with herself. On the outside, she is nothing but pleasant, kindly engaging the people around her, commenting favorably on their dress and conversation. But on the inside, we hear something different. Ruthlessly, and with a keen sense of her own superiority, Mrs. Turpin judges everyone in the room. When a lady tells her that she had bought some "joo-ry" with green stamps, Mrs. Turpin says to herself: "Ought to have got you a wash rag and some soap."[5] And when a young woman whom she finds particularly disagreeable is described as having been to college up north, Mrs. Turpin mutters, "Well, it hasn't done much for her manners."[6] Another woman in the waiting room comments disparagingly on Mrs. Turpin's hog farm: "Hogs. Nasty stinking things, a-gruntin' and a-rootin' all over the place," and the protagonist protests that her hogs are actually quite clean — and then thinks to herself while casting a furtive glance to her left: "cleaner by far than that child."[7]

All of this comes to a head when Mrs. Turpin utters a soliloquy of gratitude for all the gifts that God has given her: "If it's one thing I am it's grateful. When I think who all I could have been besides myself and what all I got, a little of everything and a good disposition besides, I just feel like shouting 'Thank you, Jesus, for making everything the way it is!'"[8] With that, a book hits her directly over her left eye. It had been hurled by the unmannered college girl who now was on Mrs. Turpin, her fingers digging into the soft flesh of our hero's throat. The doctor and nurse scramble into action, pulling the crazed young woman away and giving her a shot to sedate her. But before she drifts into unconsciousness, the girl locks Mrs. Turpin in a fierce stare, and it occurs to Mrs. Turpin that this ugly and violent woman *knows* her "in some intense and personal way." Half-fascinated and half-terrified, the older woman asks in a hoarse voice, "What you got to say to me?" Continuing to stare into Mrs. Turpin's face with an awful concentration, the young woman says, "Go back to hell where you came from you old wart hog."[9] Despite the vociferous protestations of the others in the room, Mrs. Turpin realizes, in some uncanny but definitive way, that the girl was right, that her words carried the force of a revelation. As the violent college student is carried away, we learn her name: "Mary-Grace."

Very much like the Pharisee in Jesus' parable who publicly thanked God for not making him like other men, Mrs. Turpin had rejoiced in a sense of her moral superiority. And it was upon this sense that her relationship with God was based. Like a terrapin (how like Turpin!), she had encased herself in a carapace of self-righteousness, and it required the ministrations of God's grace (Mary-Grace) to break through that protective shell. What is wonderful is that Mrs. Turpin begins to walk the road of sanctity only after that devastating revelation. At the end of the story, she stands outside of her hog pen and looks up into the evening sky and spies a purple streak. As a visionary light sparkled in her eyes "she saw the streak as a vast swinging bridge extending upward from the earth. . . . Upon it a vast horde of souls were rumbling toward heaven. There were whole companies of white-trash, clean for the first time in their lives, and bands of black niggers in white robes, and battalions of freaks and lunatics shouting and clapping and leaping like frogs." Taking up the rear of the procession were people like herself and her husband — proper, dignified, sure of themselves — but she saw, "by their shocked and altered faces that even their virtues were being burned away."[10] All of the people that she had judged to be inferior were leading the unruly parade of the saints. Her people were there, but they were in the back, a little stunned to be in such company and feeling naked and exposed, the shield of their virtues gone. Saints are not those who are free from sin; they are those who have the humility and grace to join the parade of redeemed sinners.

As we saw, the first words out of the mouth of Jesus in the Gospel of Mark are a call to conversion: "The kingdom of God has come near. Repent and believe in the Good News" (Mark 1:15). The life, preaching, and mission of Jesus are predicated upon the assumption that all is not well with us, that we stand in need of *metanoia,* a renovation of vision, attitude and behavior. A few decades ago the book *I'm OK — You're OK* appeared. Its title, and the attitude that it embodies, are inimical to Christianity. Anthony de Mello answered that book with a better motto: "I'm an ass and so are you!" A salvation religion makes no sense if all is basically fine with us, if all we need is a little sprucing up around the edges. Christian saints are those who can bear the awful revelation that sin is not simply an abstraction or something that other people wrestle with, but a power that lurks and works in them. And this is why knowing that we are sinners — even wart hogs from hell — is the second path of holiness.

The Nature of Sin

So the project is knowing that we are sinners, but what, exactly, is sin? This is a much more difficult question than it seems, because sin is a negativity, a dysfunction, and hence cannot be looked at directly. Henri de Lubac spoke of it as *cette claudication mystérieuse,* this mysterious limp, and thereby caught its elusive, derivative, and parasitic quality.[11] We might begin to shed some light on the issue by distinguishing, in accord with biblical instincts, between Sin and sins, that is to say, between the underlying disease and its many symptoms. When, at the end of his career, the Curé d'Ars was asked what wisdom he had gained about human nature from his many years of hearing confessions, he responded, "people are much sadder than they seem." Blaise Pascal rests his apologetic for

Christianity on the simple fact that all people are unhappy.[12] This universal, enduring, and stubborn sadness is Sin. Now this does not mean that Sin is identical to psychological depression. The worst sinners can be the most psychologically well-adjusted people, and the greatest saints can be, by any ordinary measure, quite unhappy. When I speak of sadness in this context, I mean the deep sense of unfulfillment. We want the Truth and we get it, if at all, in dribs and drabs; we want the Good, and we achieve it only rarely; we seem to know what we ought to be, but we are in fact something else. This spiritual frustration, this inner warfare, this debility of soul, is Sin.

It is nowhere better described than in the seventh chapter of the letter that Paul wrote to the Romans toward the end of his life. The passage begins simply and magnificently: "I do not understand my own actions" (Rom. 7:14). Paul knows, even twenty years after his conversion to Christ, that he remains an enigma to himself. And the mystery is clearly articulated: "For I do not do what I want, but I do the very thing I hate" (Rom. 7:15). Paul lives at cross purposes to himself, his best inclinations stymied, his highest thoughts countered by his lowest desires, his good will giving rise to sordid acts. Sounding like an alcoholic who knows that taking a drink is the very worst thing he could do precisely as he raises the glass to his lips, Paul continues, "I can will what is right, but I cannot do it" (Rom. 7:18). When he looks within, he sees, not an ordered harmony, but a battlefield: "for I delight in the law of God in my inmost self, but I see in my members another law at war with the law of my mind" (Rom. 7:23). And the conclusion of this bit of brutally honest introspection is an anguished statement and an equally anguished question: "Wretched man that I am! Who will rescue me from this body of death?" (Rom. 7:24). The Apostle to the Gentiles needs no Mrs. Turpin–like awakening, for he sees the truth of his situation with awful clarity: his spiritual life is a civil war, and no amount of fighting will resolve the conflict.

Pascal mines further this Pauline vein when he says, "We are incapable of not desiring truth and happiness and incapable of either certainty or happiness."[13] This is both our greatness (we know what we ought to have) and our wretchedness (we cannot achieve it). In one of the best known of his *Pensées*, Pascal says, "Man is neither angel nor beast, and it is unfortunately the case that anyone trying to act the angel acts the beast."[14] In other words, when we convince ourselves that all is basically well with us and that through our efforts of mind, will, imagination, can work our way out of our wretchedness, we do not resolve our dysfunction; we intensify it. Part of the mythology of the Enlightenment was just this confidence in auto-salvation. Many nineteenth-century thinkers, including some Christians, held that our technological advances, our improvements in medicine, our growing political wisdom would conduce, finally, to the emergence of the kingdom. The prophets from Kierkegaard to Barth pointed out the dangerous hubris behind this assumption, and the horrors of the twentieth century — two global wars, several attempts at genocide, the nuclear threat, and the beginning of terrorism — have shown the truth of Pascal's dictum. The perpetrators of the greatest violence in human history were not those who believed in the fall but precisely those who denied it.

Every Advent Christians sing a haunting song whose words and tune go back to the ninth century, but I wonder how carefully they aver to the lyrics:

> O come, O come, Emmanuel,
> and ransom captive Israel
> that mourns in lonely exile here
> until the Son of God appears.

In the ancient world, people were tremendously afraid of being kidnapped and held for ransom. Alone, far from home, malnourished, often tortured, hostages could only hope against hope that their deliverance might come. This is the situation evoked by that well-known song: Israel, the people of God, are held for ransom in their lonely exile, and they cry out for their savior, the Son of God. To be in Sin is to know the truth and to feel the texture of this imprisonment.

In his homilies on the book of Exodus, Origen proposes an allegorical reading of the battle between the children of Israel and the Egyptians.[15] The Israelites, he says, symbolize all of the positive powers of the soul — creativity, intelligence, energy, love — while Pharaoh (and his minions) stand for the negative forces of fear, hatred, and violence. What has happened in our fallen state is that Pharaoh has come to dominate Israel, that is to say, the power of Sin has co-opted and mastered for its purposes our positive energies. Now our minds (which remain hungry for the Truth) are placed in service of falsity; and our wills (which still love the Good) are pressed into service for evil; and our creativity (which still longs for the beautiful) is harnessed to ugly purposes. According to Exodus, Pharaoh compels the Israelites to build fortified cities and monuments to himself. And so, following the allegory, our sinner's souls are given over to producing fortifications to protect the ego and monuments to trumpet its prominence. This enslavement of our best to our worst is Sin.

Augustine offers one of the pithiest definitions of Sin: it is the state of being *incurvatus in se* (caved in on oneself). The powers of the soul, which are meant to orient us to nature and other human beings and the cosmos and finally the infinite mystery of God, are focused in on the tiny and infinitely uninteresting ego. Like a black hole, the sinful soul draws all of the light and energy around it into itself. Dante illustrates this Augustinian insight by placing Satan at the pit of Hell, frozen in ice, incapable of movement, and weeping from all six of his eyes.[16] The Devil's angel wings (now devolved into unsightly bat wings) beat the air furiously, but he can go nowhere: "I can will what is right, but I cannot do it." Trying to fly while stuck in the ice; driving your car with one foot on the gas and the other on the brake: that is the dysfunction, the frustration, that the Bible calls "Sin."

But we mustn't despair, even after surveying this depressing series of images and metaphors, for we have a savior. We cannot set this condition right ("who will deliver me from this body of death?"), but there is someone who can. Paul's lament ends with an exultant proclamation: "Thanks be to God through Jesus Christ our Lord!" (Rom. 7:25). Christianity affirms that Emmanuel (God with us) has come and has gone right to the bottom of Sin in order

to defeat it. In his full humanity, Jesus entered into the complex
nexus of Sin, and in his full divinity, he did something about it.
He stood shoulder to shoulder with us in the muddy Jordan waters
of our egotism, but he was not simply a fellow sufferer. He also
lifted us out of those waters and offered us transfiguration. And it
is none other than those so lifted up and so transfigured that can
look with confidence, and even a touch of humor, at the mess from
which they are being saved. It is the saints who know that they are
sinners.

Dante's *Purgatorio*

And so, strengthened and illumined by our redemption, we walk
the second path. This way is, necessarily, a painful one, but there
is no substitute for it: like the soldier's boot camp or the patient's
surgery, it has to be gone through. We have to *know* that we are
sinners, not in the abstract Cartesian sense, but in the more classical sense of experiencing through intimacy. We have to smell the
stench and taste the acidity and touch the rough texture of our
sin. There is no more thorough narrative in our tradition of this
painful and liberating process than Dante's *Divine Comedy,* and it
would thus behoove us to spend some time with this great text in
order to delineate the contours of the second path of holiness.

The poem opens with an awakening:

> Midway along the journey of our life
> I awoke to find myself in a dark wood
> for I had wandered off from the straight path.[17]

Though Dante describes this moment as almost unspeakably painful, it is, like Paul's experience on the road to Damascus, an event
of the greatest spiritual power. Dante awakens from his ego-centric
slumber, discovers that he is lost, and is thus enabled to commence
the process of purification. Glancing up and catching sight of a
mountain bathed in light, he is filled with hope, realizing that the
climbing of that height will be his salvation. He eagerly sets out,
but his ascent is blocked by three beasts: a leopard, a lion, and a

she-wolf, evocative of three types of sin — incontinence, violence, and fraudulence. What he comes to see is that he cannot race up the mountain of salvation without honestly confronting all of those energies within him that led him off the right road. In his despair, he cries out to heaven, and his prayer is heard by Mary, the Mother of God, who in turn calls to Lucia, the patroness of light and vision, who in turn summons Beatrice, Dante's ideal love who had died when still a very young woman. These three women — symbolic of compassion and gentleness — thus preside over our hero's spiritual renovation, the softening of his crusty self-absorption. Concerned lest her friend be permanently lost, Beatrice calls to the Roman poet Virgil, who is languishing in Limbo, to come forward and assist Dante. And so appears this venerable figure — so much like Dante himself — who will guide our lost soul on his journey. The ancient poet tells his medieval counterpart that there is a way out of his despair but that he must pay a high price; before coming to the light, he must make a pilgrimage through Hell (in order to see his own sin) and then up the mount of Purgatory (in order to cleanse him of his impurity).[18] He must walk the second path.

And so down he goes through the various levels of Hell, forced to witness the agonies of the damned and to see in them the suffering of his own cramped soul. The atmosphere of Hell is stifling and claustrophobic (like the spirit that is caved in on itself), and the attitude of its citizens is sad, frightened, and fiercely individualistic. When Dante shrinks from a particularly horrible sight or swoons, Virgil shows no mercy: he berates him and rouses him to look. When he has withstood it all, finally seeing sad Satan at the very bottom, he has completed the first phase of the pilgrimage and is ready for the second, the purgation of his various dysfunctions. This will take place on the mount of Purgatory that surges up out of the south sea on the far side of the earth.

Still guided by Virgil, Dante emerges from the gloom of Hell and spies the distinctive constellations of the southern hemisphere as well as the planet Venus.[19] This reminds him that the journey he will now undertake must be directed by powers outside of himself — just as ships are guided by the stars — and that the lodestar must be love. The sufferings on Purgatory will be, for the most part, as intense as those of Hell, but with this difference: the former are accepted out of love — and hence become redemptive — while the latter are resisted and thus remain meaningless.[20] Before he can begin his climb, his face is washed of the grime of Hell and he is girded with a reed. Many commentators have taken this latter detail as symbolic, first, of the humility required of the penitent, and second, of the flexibility he will need in order to bend with punishment and not break. To walk the second path of holiness is a humbling and somewhat harrowing business, and we who would walk it must lay aside our arrogant self-regard and resistance to the divine assault.

A somewhat surprising feature of the *Purgatorio* is the amount of time that Dante and Virgil spend in "ante-purgatory," a sort of holding area occupied by those who are waiting to begin the climb of the mount. Here they meet souls who, for a variety of reasons, put off the hard interior work of the spirit too long and who are compelled now, through a kind of law of karma, to wait. Some of these were very good people in life, active and productive, but their busy-ness masked a slothfulness of the soul. And so in ante-purgatory, they learn the discipline of silence and inactivity, the quietude that is required for spiritual ferment. Almost a third of the *Purgatorio* is spent describing this vestibule, and Dante's reader naturally becomes impatient, eager to get to the heart of the matter, the rhythm of the text itself thereby mimicking the discipline of the place.

A key theme that runs all through the *Purgatorio* is sounded for the first time in ante-purgatory: those on the way to salvation pray for and encourage one another. This is just the opposite of the style of Hell, where each sufferer finds his fellow a further torture. We recall from the first section that when we have found the center in God, we have discovered the point that links us to everything and everyone else in the cosmos. Hence, from there, your good is my good and vice versa. What comes to mind here is Augustine's magnificent definition of heaven as *totus Christus amans seipsum* (the total Christ loving himself). Paul told us in First Corinthians that if we have not love we are nothing; Purgatory is a training in love, the formation of the Body of Christ.

After their period of waiting, Dante and Virgil come to Peter's Gate, the portal to the mount of Purgatory proper. Before its great bronze door are three steps, colored white, black, and red.[21] These stand for the three attitudes of the repentant soul: confession, contrition, and satisfaction. In the brightly polished white of the first step, sinners see themselves with clarity and uncompromising honesty; in the black of the second step, they appreciate the hard, grinding work of contrition, feeling the pain that sin has caused themselves and others; and in the red of the third step, they sense the work of satisfaction that must be done. Acknowledging sin is not enough; restitution must be made in order that justice (right order) might be restored. The word "satisfaction" comes from the Latin *satis facere,* literally, to make enough, to do the required work.

An interesting detail: the souls doing their purgatorial work release *themselves* from bondage, because only they know when satisfaction has been done. In the film *The Mission,* Mendoza, a mercenary and slave trader, murders his brother in a jealous rage. Overwhelmed with guilt, he sits in a squalid cell, refusing to communicate or eat. The Jesuit missionary Fr. Gabriel challenges him with brutal directness, and Mendoza agrees to accompany him to his mission deep in the jungle. But the murderer resolves, as a penance, to drag behind him a terribly heavy bundle containing the accoutrements of his former life — swords, helmets, muskets, and the like. Through jungle, over mountains, up streams, the poor man drags this load, until his fellow travelers have had enough. They beg Fr. Gabriel, saying, "We think he has taken this far enough." The priest responds, "But *he* doesn't think so, and until he does, I don't think so either." Only when he has lugged his penitential burden up a steep cliffside and arrived at the mission does Mendoza relent. When the bundle is cut away, he breaks down in tears both remorseful and joyful: finally *he* knew that satisfaction had been made. This is Dante's third step of red.

As he enters the purgation process, Dante receives the mark of seven "P's" on his forehead, a sign of the seven deadly *peccata* (sins), the principal manifestations of Sin.[22] So many of the spiritual masters have taught that our sins are much more visible to others than to ourselves, as are these letters on Dante's forehead. This is one reason, by the way, why it is good to love our enemies: their hatred is the mirror in which we can see our own dysfunction. Humble, flexible, ready to suffer in love, our pilgrim now enters the seven-story mountain of Purgatory (the inspiration, of course, for Thomas Merton's autobiography). On each level or cornice of the mountain, he will witness those being purged of one of the seven deadly sins: pride, envy, anger, sloth, avarice, gluttony, and lust. And this makes his journey a particularly apt display of our second path of holiness.

On the first story, he meets the prideful, those who were burdened in life by the heaviest and most serious of the deadly sins. What, precisely, is pride? It really has little to do with ostentatious haughtiness or vigorous self-promotion, for the quietest and most inconspicuous person can be full of pride. Pride, essentially, is self-regard. And this means, not so much thinking highly of oneself, but simply *looking* at oneself. Perhaps it is best illustrated by contrasting two experiences. Consider first: you are lost in a fascinating conversation, following the central idea as it unfolds, compelled by the rhythm of question and answer, unaware of any "agenda" of your own or of your interlocutor. And second: you are watching yourself have a conversation, conscious of the effect you are producing and want to produce, exquisitely attentive to the reactions and attitudes of your conversation partner, hoping that she finds you interesting, suave, and intelligent.[23] In the first case, you are ecstatic, literally outside of yourself, immersed in the density of being; in the second case, you are cut off from being, or better, you have drawn it into the narrow corridors of your own consciousness (*curvatus in se*). In the first instance, your soul is like a seed that has cracked open and mixed with its environment; in the second, it is like a seed that remains closed tight. Norman Mailer once described the experience of watching Richard Nixon in characteristically awkward action: it is as though, he said, there were a little Nixon poised just alongside the head of the big Nixon, carefully pulling levers and making commands, "smile, look concerned, laugh, make your argument." Whether this is a fair description of the former president is, for our purposes, beside the point, but it does illustrate beautifully what the spiritual masters mean by pride: the self-regard that prevents ecstasy.

Now what is the antidote to pride? On most of the cornices, the sinners are punished through a sort of enantiadromia — a running in the opposite direction. Aristotle said that if the stick is bent to the right and we want to straighten it out, we have to bend it back dramatically to the left. And Ignatius of Loyola recommends that the practitioners of his Spiritual Exercises *agere contra* (act in the contrary direction of their sin). So the prideful are forced to carry huge slabs of rock on their backs, the effort pressing them down to the earth. There is a twofold symbolism here. On the one hand, since they spent their lives looking at themselves, they are now forced down to the ground, that is to say, to the dense particularity of being. They are humbled (from the Latin *humus*, the earth), not as an arbitrary punishment, but as a spiritual practice. In their pride, they lived in a kind of ethereal, unreal atmosphere; their purgation is, consequently, a rather brutal immersion in the real. The other dimension of the symbolism is this: pride is a terrible burden. When I am compelled to look at myself at every moment, I can never give myself away; it is though I carry a great weight on my back that precludes the possibility of ecstasy. In his essay "John Ruskin" Chesterton wrote, "The humble man will be always talkative; for he is interested in his subject and knows that it is best shown in talk. But the proud man will be generally silent; for he is not interested in his subject but in himself." In other words, voluble persons, though they might be embarrassing themselves by saying the wrong thing, at least are out of themselves, lost in the conversation. Quiet persons, though safe, remain imprisoned. In a similar vein, Anthony de Mello proposed the following parable to describe us prideful souls. A group of people sit on a bus that is passing through the most glorious countryside, but they have the shades pulled down on all the windows and are bickering about who gets front seat on the bus.[24] This is the burden of pride: preferring the narrow and stuffy confines of the bus to the beauty that is effortlessly available all around. This, of course, is why Jesus can say, "My yoke is easy and my burden is light" (Matt. 11:30). What the Lord proposes is, not a freedom from suffering, but, what is much more important, a freedom from the self. Dante's prideful souls are reminded of the heavy burden as they lumber around the first cornice of purgatory.

On the next level, the envious are disciplined. This cornice is unadorned, stark. And the penitents are dressed in the simplest of garb, something like monastic robes. But the most striking detail emerges only when Dante takes a close look at them: their eyelids are sewn shut with iron thread "like falcons newly caught / whose eyes we stitch to tame their restlessness."[25] It is as though these sinners are meant not to look at anything at all. Now this can seem a bit puzzling in the light of our previous discussion. Wasn't humility described precisely as the capacity to look out at the world, free from self-preoccupation? It is important to note that Dante is following the medieval masters who speak of envy as a close relative of pride. Envy is looking out at the world, but not in self-forgetting wonder; instead, it looks out and compares what it sees with what the ego has. Therefore, it is not ecstatic vision, but an anxious and resentful vision that only intensifies the agony of pride.

The novelist Gore Vidal, in an acid but wonderfully honest remark, observed, "When a friend of mind succeeds, something in me dies." That is the voice of pure envy. The success of another diminishes the ego caught in the zero-sum game of spiritual competition; when someone else's reputation rises, mine must fall. And of course this works in the opposite direction, giving rise to what the Germans call *Schadenfreude* (the pleasure at another's pain). Thus we could turn Vidal's observation around: "When a friend of mine fails, something in me comes to life." We notice, by the way, the exquisiteness of the envy Vidal describes, signaled by the "friend" who is the point of comparison. Those who are closest to us are also those with whom we most readily play the game of competition and hence those of whom we are most easily envious.

When we examine the scriptural witness, we find almost everywhere evidence of just this phenomenon. Cain is jealous of his brother Abel; Jacob is envious of his twin, Esau; Joseph's brothers are envious of their brother's special status; Saul resents David, the young man he had invited into his household; the other disciples are envious of James and John. Envy — especially among close friends and family — is arguably *the* driving force behind the drama of the scriptural narrative. And therefore we see the wisdom in Dante's harsh punishment. Since the envious person's problem is the addiction to looking fearfully, resentfully, violently at the other, his penance is a sort of imposed blindness.

The deepest antidote to envy, the *agere contra,* is admiration. A basic truth of Christian spirituality is this: *no one is owed anything.* Creation is the act by which God gives rise, every moment, to the totality of the finite world. Because God makes literally everything *ex nihilo,* nothing in the universe has a claim on its existence; rather, everything that exists holds its being as a gift. And therefore when we complain that we are not receiving the praise or the attention or the status that we deserve, we are speaking ontological nonsense. In light of the sheer gratuitousness of creation, the only proper response to existence is one of gratitude and admiration. Since no one deserves anything, all beauty and goodness that we see, in ourselves or in someone else, ought simply to be appreciated — and neither clung to nor resented.

A neat Dantean touch is that on each level of Purgatory, the sinners are met by a Marian counterexample. Thus the prideful hear the story of Mary's humble acquiescence to the divine will at the Annunciation, "Let it be done to me according to thy word." And the envious are reminded of the wedding feast at Cana, where Mary looked out at the misfortune of the newly married couple who had run out of wine and experienced, not *Schadenfreude,* but a rush of compassion, saying to her Son, "They have no more wine."[26]

On the next level of the mountain, Virgil and Dante meet the angry. It is important to note that, just as the more grievous sins are punished as one descends into Hell, so the less grievous sins are addressed as one climbs the mount of Purgatory. Pride for the medievals is the worst sin, since it turns us decisively away from the ultimate good who is God, and envy, a close relative of pride, is derivatively evil inasmuch as it focuses on the harming of another person. Anger, punished on the third cornice, is a less serious matter, because the passion of anger *can* be directed positively. This takes place, Thomas Aquinas tells us, when one seeks the righting of a wrong in an ordered and moderate way.[27] Thus the person who is filled with righteous indignation (think of Jesus cleansing the Temple or railing against the scribes and Pharisees) experiences the passion of anger but under the discipline of justice. This clarification is especially important given our psychological culture's insistence on the "owning" and free expression of feelings. Many therapies — from ordinary psychoanalysis to primal scream — call for the patients to discover and give voice to their anger. Neither Aquinas nor Dante would necessarily quarrel with this, since it amounts to an acknowledgment that one has been hurt or wronged in some way and a feeling of the negative passion that this has aroused.

But the *sin* of anger is the lust for vengeance untethered to reason. It is not simply sensing the indignation of injustice; it is acting on this sensation disproportionately, allowing passion to cloud judgment. How easy it would have been for Martin Luther King to have surrendered to sinful anger, given the history of hatred that his people had lived through. Part of his genius and sanctity was precisely his stubborn connecting of his people's anger with a keen sense of transcendent justice. In a speech in Montgomery, Alabama, in 1965, King told his listeners who, in their eagerness to set things right, were becoming impatient: "The arm of the moral universe is long, but it bends toward justice."[28] And, after his home had been attacked, King informed an angry crowd of blacks who had gathered for vengeance that they must love their persecutors even as they hate what they have done. King knew that passion without righteousness (the *sin* of anger) is a short road to both moral and political chaos.

What is disconcerting, of course, is how rare King's witness and praxis are both on the world stage and in interpersonal relations.

In Ireland, Rwanda, the Holy Land, Indonesia, China, Russia, the United States — anger is passed on from generation to generation like a bacillus. Never forgetting, never forgiving, never recovering from past offenses, peoples around the globe allow their lust for vengeance to well up unchecked. And the same phenomenon can be seen in families and communities where grudges are borne for decades, even when the originating offense is long forgotten. And here is where we must challenge our emotions-worshiping culture: when reason is clouded over, the claiming and expressing of feeling is not the solution but the problem.

The punishment meted out to the angry is, in light of these reflections, altogether appropriate: they are tormented by a thick smoke that stings their eyes and burns their throats. In the midst of his sober analysis of anger, Aquinas quotes Gregory the Great's surprisingly vivid description of someone in the grip of anger: "the heart goaded by the pricks of anger is convulsed, the body trembles, the tongue entangles itself, the face is inflamed, the eyes are enraged and fail utterly to recognize those whom we know; the tongue makes sounds indeed, but there is no sense in its utterance."[29] Sinful anger is a passion that obscures correct vision, compromises clear thinking, and precludes honest and helpful communication; it contorts and confounds, turning the angry person into a bit of a cartoon caricature of a human being. The sinners on Dante's third level are meant to experience this contortion.

The Marian counterexample is, as always, instructive. When Mary, after her desperate search, discovered her son amid the doctors in the Temple, she was relieved, but undoubtedly hurt and confused. She must have felt that a kind of injustice had been done to her and her husband. Yet she responds with the meek question: "Didn't you know that your father and I have been looking for you?" and she accepts his response, "Did you not know that I must be about my Father's business," thus placing her anger in the context of a higher order.

Our searching moral inventory continues as Dante and Virgil come to the fourth level of Mount Purgatory. Here, at the very center of the mount — and the midpoint of the literary architecture of the *Divine Comedy* — the slothful are punished. We have arrived, as it were, to the dead center, and it is therefore appropriate that we look at those who sinned through a lack of spiritual energy.[30] For the medievals, movement is indispensable. All things have come forth from God through creation and now, guided by providence, they are being led back to God. Therefore the restless longing of the soul, the straining toward God of mind, body, and will, is the heart of the matter. What undermines and blocks this process is the sin that Dante calls "sloth," spiritual laziness.

And perhaps this is why Karl Barth called sloth in fact the deadliest of the deadly sins. When we are running aggressively away from God, there is a good chance that we will collapse and move back in the right direction, but when we are simply stuck, complacent in our spiritual shallowness, neither hot nor cold, then we are in far greater moral danger. We must note that the sin of sloth can be unrelated to the torpor or laziness of the body. Physical lethargy can be one of its symptoms, but in point of fact, a bustling, busy-ness can be a cover for a profound slackness of spirit. Dorothy Sayers described sloth this way: "it is that whole poisoning of the will which, beginning with indifference and an attitude of 'I couldn't care less' extends to the deliberate refusal of joy and culminates in morbid introspection and despair."[31] Can we see this attitude writ large in the secularized culture of our time? Once God has been rendered so transcendent as to be irrelevant, the desacralized world tends to rest in itself, finally indifferent to things spiritual, all too willing collectively to sigh, "I couldn't care less" about life, death, immortality, God's will. This flattened-out boredom of the soul is sloth.

How are these sinners punished? They have to run! Like today's health club devotees on their treadmills, Dante's slothful race incessantly around the fourth circle of Purgatory. As a group of runners pass Dante, he hears them shout, "Mary in haste ran to the hills." The Gospel of Luke tells us that when Mary received the message that she was to be the mother of God, she "proceeded in haste" into the hill country of Judea in order to tell her cousin Elizabeth (Luke 1:39). Zeal for the mission, a passion to communicate the word, consumed her, and all of her energies of soul and body were roused to action. This is the Marian counterexample to sloth.

Cardinal Joseph Bernardin, the late archbishop of Chicago, often told the story of how he was rescued from sloth. When he was archbishop of Cincinnati, president of the National Conference of Catholic Bishops and one of the most respected church leaders in America, he was confronted by a group of young priests from his diocese. They told him that he was not sufficiently focused in his spiritual life, not a man of prayer. At first he was insulted that these men, some of whom he had ordained, would challenge the dedication of their spiritual father, but then he realized the truth of the accusation: behind his frenetic — and remarkably successful — activity on behalf of the church, there lurked a lazy soul. And so, under the guidance of these same young clergy, Bernardin set himself the task of praying for an hour at the beginning of each day — no matter how tired or busy or distracted he was. This discipline, he said, changed his life.

As is well known, at the end of his life, Cardinal Bernardin faced two enormous crosses: the accusation of sexual misconduct (of which he was exonerated) and the onset of the pancreatic cancer that would eventually kill him. Through both ordeals, he walked with an honesty, goodness, sense of humor, and spirit of forgiveness that profoundly edified both church and society. That he handled these crises with such grace and equanimity Bernardin attributed to that daily hour of prayer. He proved to be such a powerful figure at the end of his life precisely because a few of his brother priests had told him, in the midst of his sloth, to get up and run.

The next deadly sin that Virgil and Dante encounter is avarice, the inordinate love of the material goods of this world. This is a sin that seems to have particularly bothered Dante, since the *Inferno* and the *Purgatorio* are filled with pathetic people — often clerics and popes — who practiced it.[32] We have spoken before of *concupiscentia,* the errant and confused desire for God which, in a certain sense, underlies all expressions of sin. We want the infinity of God, but we hook that desire onto a finite object; and the result, inevitably, is addiction, running around and around that object obsessively, locked in a hopeless quest for a satisfaction that it cannot possibly give. With regard to avarice, this dynamic appears with particular clarity. This amount of money, this house, this car, this suit of clothes are never enough — and so we want more money, a bigger house, a sportier car, a more fashionable outfit. And then, in time, those will prove unsatisfactory, and the addictive pattern will play itself out again.

In his customarily pithy way, Thomas Aquinas spells out the irrationality that undergirds avarice. Money, says Thomas, is valuable only inasmuch as it procures material things, and material things are valuable only in the measure that they satisfy certain bodily longings. Consequently, neither money nor material objects can, themselves, be the ultimate object of the will, that which finally brings joy, since they are subordinate to ends outside of themselves. The problem with avaricious persons is, in a word, that they confuse ends and means.[33]

There is a connection between this Thomistic analysis of avarice and Karl Marx's reading of the alienating effects of capitalism. For Marx, the principal problem with a capitalist political economy is not primarily structural but psychological. When seen as a means of exchange, money is perfectly natural and helpful, but when it is sought obsessively for its own sake, when material commodities are subordinated to it, then money transmutes into capital. It is this *Kapital* that, according to Marx, reigns as the "non-sensuous god" of a capitalist society and exerts an hypnotic and psychologically debilitating influence at all of its levels. In the *Economic and Philosophical Manuscripts of 1844*, we find this remarkable passage: "The less you eat, drink and read books; the less you go to the theatre, the dance hall, the public house; the less you think, love, theorize, sing, paint, fence, etc. the more you save, the greater becomes your treasure which neither moths nor dust will devour — your capital. The less you are, the more you have."[34] For both Aquinas and Marx, the preoccupation with money is a kind of psychological illness or, at the very least, an intellectual misperception. Having must always be subordinate to being.

What is the punishment for the avaricious? They are pressed down to the ground and held there in place, unable to move:

> When I came out and stood on the Fifth Round
> I saw spirits stretched out upon the dust, lying face
> downward, all of them in tears.[35]

When Dante asks one of the sufferers — it turns out to be Pope Adrian V — the meaning for this discipline, he receives this answer:

> Just as our eyes, attached to worldly goods
> would never leave the earth to look above
> so Justice here has forced them to the ground.[36]

As the angry were made to feel the pain of their dysfunction, so the avaricious have their faces, quite literally, rubbed in theirs. The immobility of these sinners calls to mind the immobility of Satan, stuck in the ice at the pit of Hell. The soul is meant to soar into God; but the love of earthly things pins it to the earth and radically restricts the range of its vision and movement.

The Marian example that edifies these penitents is the nativity of Christ in the humble stable at Bethlehem. The Mother of God demanded neither palatial surroundings nor bodily comfort while she played her central role in the theo-drama. There is a connection here to mission as well: the avaricious person — weighed down by the goods of the world — is unable to move when and how God demands. Just as the tennis player has to be fit and agile in order to respond to the unpredictable movement of the ball, so the spiritual seeker has to be "light on her feet," unencumbered, if she is to answer the unpredictable call of God. Precisely because she was so unattached, Mary could get up and hurry to Egypt with the Christ child when that was required of her.

As Dante and Virgil come toward the summit of Mount Purgatory, their traveling becomes easier, since the weightiness of sin is gradually falling off of them. The last two deadly sins — gluttony and lust — are the lightest and least serious of the seven, because they are more a disorder of the appetites than a perversion of the mind or will. On the sixth cornice, Dante meets the souls of the gluttonous, and he immediately sees how they have been punished through a frightful emaciation:

> Their eyes dark-shadowed, sunken in their heads
> their faces pale, their bodies worn so thin
> that every bone was molded to their skin.[37]

They are also compelled to sing a passage from Psalm 51: "O Lord open my lips, and my mouth shall declare your praise." This is to signal that the opening of the mouth is not only for the taking in of food and drink, but also for the announcing of God's goodness.

Hunger and thirst are two of the most pressing desires we have. For most of us, to go for a day without food or water would be almost unbearable; indeed no human being could live for more than a few days without some sustenance. We eat a huge meal and tell ourselves that we will never eat again, but then, within hours, that familiar emptiness returns, and we are once more sniffing and looking for food. Hunger and thirst are thus like little children who insistently clamor to have their needs met. If we indulge them too liberally, they will, precisely because of their power, come to dominate the soul completely. And when this happens, the deeper hungers for the truth, for justice, for lasting relationship, for intimacy with God, never have a chance to surface. And this is why gluttony is a spiritual danger.

The lust for sensuous pleasure can become so great that zeal for the mission is occluded; and this is how the devil first tempts Jesus in the desert: "If you are the Son of God, command these stones to become loaves of bread" (Matt. 4:3). He urges him, in other words, to use his powers in order to scratch the itch of sensual desire rather than to do the will of his Father. But Jesus counters by naming the spiritual need far more elemental than any physical compulsion: "One does not live by bread alone but by every word that comes from the mouth of God" (Matt. 4:4).

In his "Essay on the Development of Christian Doctrine," John Henry Newman spells out the nine principles that undergird a vibrantly Christian view of the world. Along with such principles as

Incarnation, sacramentality, grace, and sin, Newman lists asceticism, that is to say, the "disciplining of our lower nature."[38] This has nothing to do with a pleasure-denying puritanism or a dislike of the body. Rather, it is grounded in a keen sense that physical wants can be overemphasized and hence conflict with the energies of the spirit. Accordingly, Christians know that asceticism in food and drink is a structuring element of the practice of their faith. And this is the *agere contra* practiced, as we've come to expect, in somewhat exaggerated form, by the gluttonous on Mount Purgatory. These famished souls seem to open their lips only for the praise of God.

The last stop on the journey up the mountain is at the cornice where the lustful are punished. For those who were formed in a Jansenist-flavored Catholicism or a puritanical Protestantism, it might seem more than a bit surprising that the least serious of the deadly sins, according to Dante, is lust. It is perhaps disturbing but undoubtedly true that when the words "sin" or "morality" are used today, what springs to the minds of many (if not most) Christians, is something to do with sexuality. And when politicians speak of "family values," they usually have sexually related issues in mind. But this sex-obsession is far from the mind of Dante. As we have seen, pride, envy, and anger are, for him, far worse offenses against God, far more dangerous distortions of the soul.

And there is certainly no reticence during Dante's Middle Ages to speak of sex or even to use it as a metaphor for the spiritual life. Bernard of Clairvaux (who emerges as Dante's final guide, ushering him into the presence of the Virgin Mary and the Trinity) wrote an elaborate commentary on the frankly erotic biblical book the Song of Songs. And Geoffrey Chaucer's *Canterbury Tales* — told by pilgrims to the sacred shrine of Thomas à Becket — are filled with bawdy stories and celebrations of sexual pleasure. And Thomas Aquinas taught that, due to the great harmony between body and soul before the Fall, the sex lives of Adam and Eve were especially intense and joyful. Thus, despite our own relatively purse-lipped puritanism, sexual pleasure and attraction are never to be, in themselves, confused with the sin of lust.

Lust can be defined rather simply as the use of another human being as a means to satisfy one's sexual desire. In his text on moral theology, *Love and Responsibility*, Karol Wojtyla claims that the governing principle in all moral deliberation in the arena of sex is the Kantian categorical imperative: never treat another person as a means but only as an end. In other words, the irreducible and never-to-be-compromised dignity of the individual is the great non-negotiable.[39] And this is why Wojtyla, as Pope John Paul II, could later say that lust can take place even within marriage, when one partner treats the other as less than a person.

The disorder of lust is no more dramatically and obviously on display than in the use of pornography, of which there has been an explosion in recent years. Conservative estimates are that pornography is a multibillion dollar industry in the United States alone, and its availability has increased exponentially through the Internet, a relatively safe and shame-free venue. But what has proved perhaps most disturbing is the emergence of an international sex trade involving wealthy Westerners and children, especially in third world countries. This sort of rank commodification of human beings is the ugliest consequence of lust.

The sinners on this last cornice of Purgatory are punished by being burned in fire, which is meant to remind them of the pain that their disordered sexuality has caused themselves and others. The burning drive of sexual passion can lead us to compromise even our most cherished principles and to harm our most beloved friends — and so on the mount, this burning is burned away. Anthony de Mello has said that until you can turn to the person next to you and say, "I don't need you," you are not in a position to love that person. Love, as Aquinas teaches, is willing the good of another, and not willing my own good through another. As long as I need someone, I will use that person to satisfy my own desires. It is only when I have transcended this ultimately self-centered neediness that I am in a position to will what is best for the other. When I need someone in order to calm my sexual passion, when I am in the grip of lust, I cannot possibly love.

With this final purification, Dante has completed the climb of the seven-story mountain, and now he is ready to fly. As he turns, at the summit of Purgatory, to consult with Virgil his loyal companion, he finds the Roman poet gone. Reason can take us only as far as honest introspection and purgation, but then it must give way to a surer guide. At this point, Dante's childhood love, Beatrice, evocative of divine Grace, descends from heaven in order to direct his flight through the levels of paradise. What is implied here is this: only when the will is utterly surrendered to the higher Will are real soul expansion and mission possible. The seven deadly sins are various modes of willfulness, diverse ways in which the ego blocks the deepest appropriation and activation of the center. When they are addressed, the divine Will can operate unencumbered through the human will, and it is just this paradoxical state of affairs that is signaled by Paul's "It is no longer I who live but Christ who lives in me" (Gal. 2:20) and by Isaiah's "for indeed, all we have done, you (O Lord) have done for us" (Isa. 26:12). When all of the "P's" have been wiped from his forehead, Dante is ready for the flight that is the antithesis of Satan's mournful immobility: now he can be drawn by that "power already in work in us that can do infinitely more than we can ask or imagine." With grace as his mystagogue, he is prepared to walk path three, realizing that his life is not about him. But that is to get ahead of our story.

Jesus as Judge and Savior

Just before commencing the Dante journey, we hinted that it is Christ who makes the walking of path two possible. Because we have a savior who has accompanied us all the way to the bottom of our dysfunction, we have the courage to look unblinkingly into the darkness. In this section, I would like to make this Christological connection more complete and explicit. The New Testament insists that Jesus both shows us that we are sinners (he is judge) and offers us the way out of sin (he is savior). When one or the other of these emphases is lost, the walking of the second path is decisively compromised, either through overconfidence or through terror. When they are both adequately stressed, path two opens up, because we know we *must* walk it and we *can* walk it. Let us look first at Jesus the judge.

C. S. Lewis said that Jesus came into this world like a soldier slipping clandestinely behind enemy lines.[40] He arrived, not as a conquering prince, but as the son of poor parents barely making their way in a distant outpost of the Roman Empire, and the very silence and obscurity of his coming operated as a cloak. For the world that he entered was in the grip of alien forces — the "powers and principalities" that Paul spoke of — and they brooked no opposition. Indeed, when the cover of the newborn prince was blown, the enemy revealed himself ferociously: Herod and with him all of Jerusalem trembled, and then the desperate king ordered the slaughter of all male children under the age of two in the town of Bethlehem. This is a terrible foreshadowing of the violence that would stalk Jesus his entire life.

And when, after thirty years of silence, he burst onto the public scene, Jesus awakened an opposition that was personal, societal, even cosmic in scope. The scribes and Pharisees schemed against him, his own disciples were confounded by him or at cross-purposes to him, and the demons howled in anger when he approached: "What do you have to do with us, Jesus of Nazareth? Have you come to destroy us?" (Mark 1:24). John Courtney Murray reads the Gospel of John as the story of an ever-increasing *agon* (struggle) between Jesus and his various opponents. From the relatively benign opposition of Nicodemus and the Woman at the Well, through the intellectual and verbal warfare of the Pharisees, to the explicit and brutally violent hatred of those who crucified him, Jesus faced an unrelenting battle. All of this witnesses to the *judgment* that was central to his life and work.

In Jesus of Nazareth, God's own mind became flesh, that is to say, the pattern of God's being appeared in time and space. Colossians tells us that Jesus is the "perfect image," the *eikon*, of the Father (Col. 1:15). And thus his arrival was in itself a challenge to all that is not in conformity with the divine pattern. In his very person is the kingdom, the divine *ordo*, and therefore his presence is the light in which the disorder of all the earthly kingdoms becomes apparent. In this sense, his every move, his every word, his every gesture, constituted God's judgment on the world, for in the measure that he was opposed, he clarified the dysfunctional nature of his opponents. When John the Baptist spoke of the coming of the Messiah, he used an edgy image: "His winnowing fork is in his hand, to clear his threshing floor and to gather the wheat into the granary; but the chaff he will burn with unquenchable fire" (Luke 3:17). The farmer in first-century Palestine would place the newly harvested wheat on the floor of the barn and then, using a sort of pitchfork, would toss the grain in the air, forcing the lighter chaff to separate itself from the usable wheat. Thus Jesus' presence would be a winnowing fan, an agent of separation and clarification.

And nowhere is this judgment more evident than in his violent death. Jesus did not simply pass away; he was killed, executed by command of the Roman governor and with the approval of the religious establishment. As Peter put it in the earliest kerygmatic preaching in the Acts of the Apostles: "And you killed the Author of life, whom God raised from the dead" (Acts 3:15). The implication of Peter's speech, of course, is that you, the killers, have been revealed as the enemies of life. And the "you," as Peter himself knew with special insight, included not simply the Roman and Jewish ruling classes, but everyone, even Jesus' most intimate followers. In *On Being a Christian*, Hans Küng pointed out that all the social groups of Jesus' time — Pharisees, Sadducees, Zealots, Essenes, Temple priests, Roman occupiers, Christian disciples — all had this in common: they were, at the end of the day, opposed to Jesus.[41] At the moment of truth, "they all fled." Bob Dylan said, "the enemy I see / wears the cloak of decency."[42] A favorite ruse of sinners is to wrap themselves in the mantle of respectability: Jesus the judge is the one who rips away the cloak, literally unveiling, "revealing" the truth of things. Whenever we are tempted to think that all is well with us, we hold up the cross of Jesus and let our illusions die.

But the death of Jesus is not the whole story. If it were, Christianity would be nothing more than a social movement and Jesus no more than a romantic and fondly remembered revolutionary.

On the third day after his execution, Jesus appeared alive again to his followers. Luke's account of the risen Christ's appearance to the eleven is especially instructive; he tells us that, upon seeing him, "they were startled and terrified" (Luke 24:37). This reaction is not, I submit, simply the result of seeing something unusual. In accord with the plot of most ghost stories, they are terrified because the one they abandoned and betrayed and left for dead is back — undoubtedly for revenge! As in almost all of the other accounts of the postresurrection appearances, Luke's risen Jesus does two things in the presence of his shocked followers. First, he shows them his wounds. This move is a reiteration of the judgment of the cross: don't forget, he tells them, what the world did when the Author of life appeared. A woundless Christ is embraced much more readily by his executioners, since he doesn't remind them of their crime. But the Jesus who stubbornly "shows them his hands and his side" will not permit this exculpating forgetfulness.

But then he does something else: he says, "Shalom," peace be with you (Luke 24:36). In this, he opens up a new spiritual world and thereby becomes our savior. From ancient creation myths to the Rambo and Dirty Harry movies, the principle is the same: order, destroyed through violence, is restored through a righteous exercise of greater violence. Some agent of chaos is corralled and conquered by fighting him (or it) on his own terms and overpowering him. If domination is the problem (as in the ancient stories), then a counterdomination is the solution; if gun violence is the problem (as in most cop movies), then a bigger and more skillfully handled gun is the solution. And in these myths, God or the gods are customarily invoked as the sanction for the process.[43]

And then there is Jesus. The terrible disorder of the cross (the killing of the Son of God) is addressed, not through an explosion of divine vengeance, but through a radiation of divine love. When Christ confronts those who contributed to his death, he speaks words, not of retribution, but of reconciliation and compassion. Mind you, the awful texture of the disorder is not for a moment overlooked — that is the integrity of the judgment — but the problem is resolved through nonviolence and forgiveness.

What appeared rhetorically in the Sermon on the Mount ("turn the other cheek," "love your enemies") and more concretely on the cross ("Father, forgive them, they know not what they do") now shines in all of its transfigured glory ("Shalom"). The gods who sanctioned scapegoating and the restoration of order through violence are now revealed to be phony gods, idols, projections of a sinful consciousness, and the true God comes fully into the light.

It is in this way that Jesus "takes away the sins of the world." The old schemas of handling disorder through vengeance restored a tentative and very unreliable "peace," which was really nothing but a pause between conflicts. Evil met with evil only intensifies, just as fire met with fire only increases the heat, and an "eye for an eye," as Gandhi noted, succeeds only in eventually making everyone blind. But what takes away violence is a courageous and compassionate nonviolence, just as water, the "opposite" of fire, puts out the flames. On the cross, the Son of God took on the hatred of all of us sinners, and in his forgiving love, he took that hatred away. By creating a way out of the net of our sinfulness, by doing what no mere philosopher, poet, politician, or social reformer could possibly do, Jesus saved us.

Psychologists tell us that a true friend is someone who has seen us at our worst and still loves us. If you have encountered me only on my best days, when all is going well and I am in top form, and you like me, I have no guarantee that you are my friend. But when you have dealt with me when I am most obnoxious, most self-absorbed, most afraid and unpleasant, and you still love me, then I am sure that you are my friend. The old Gospel song says, "what a friend we have in Jesus!" This is not pious sentimentalism; it is the heart of the matter. What the first Christians saw in the dying and rising of Jesus is that we killed God, and God returned in forgiving love. We murdered the Lord of Life, and he answered us, not with hatred, but with compassion. He saw us at our very worst, and loved us anyway. Thus they saw confirmed in flesh and blood what Jesus had said the night before he died: "I do not call you servants any longer . . . but I have called you friends" (John 14:15). They realized, in the drama of the Paschal Mystery, that we have not only been shown a new way; we have been drawn into a new life, a life of friendship with God.

The author of Psalm 139 wrote:

> Where can I go from your spirit?
> Or where can I flee from your presence?
> If I ascend to heaven, you are there;
> if I make my bed in Sheol, you are there.
> If I take the wings of the morning
> and settle at the farthest limits of the sea,
> even there your hand shall lead me,
> and your right hand shall hold me fast.
>
> (Ps. 139:7–10)

These words take on a new resonance and reveal their deepest significance in light of Easter. No matter where we run from God — no matter how we try to flee — God tracks us down and will not let us go. Paul Tillich read Psalm 139 as the sinner's lament, the cry of the soul who just wants to escape from the press of God: "How can I get away from you?" The answer fully disclosed in the dying and rising of Jesus is: "You can't; so stop trying." Because the Son of God has gone to the very limits of godforsakenness, we find that even as we run away from the Father, we are running directly into the arms of the Son. Unlike most contemporary New Age spiritualities, as we have seen, which emphasize the human quest for God, the biblical spirituality is the story of God's relentless search for us. And this narrative comes to its fulfillment in the recounting of God's journey into the darkest and coldest corner of human sinfulness — even into death itself — in order to find us. This divine finding, this friendship with God despite all of our efforts to avoid it, is salvation.

It is a song of salvation that Paul sings in the eighth chapter of his letter to the Romans: "For I am convinced that neither death, nor life, nor angels, nor rulers, nor things present, nor things to come, nor powers, nor height, nor depth, nor anything else in all creation, will be able to separate us from the love of God in Christ Jesus our Lord" (Rom. 8:38–39). Given God's heartbroken embrace of us at our worst, what in the entire universe could ever make us fall out of friendship with God? Paul's answer: neither time, nor space, neither the greatest nor the least, neither powers above the earth or on it or below it. This feeling of being "safe" in the divine embrace is salvation.

Thus, the wounds of Jesus, the reminders of our dysfunction, compel us to walk the second path of holiness, but the Shalom of the risen Christ, the assurance of divine friendship despite our sin, gives us the courage to walk it.

Practices for Path Two

The Confession of Sin

We recall that this is a theology of paths and practices, an embodied and exercised Christianity. What, therefore, are the practices and behaviors that keep a believer effectively adhering to the second path of holiness? What are the ways that help us "stay with" (*menein*) Jesus, judge and savior?

A first exercise is the honest confession of sin. Andrew Greeley has formulated as a law the following: "Whatever Catholics drop, someone else inevitably picks up." By most accounts, the vibrant Catholic practice of confessing one's sins simply disappeared, almost overnight, in 1967 or 1968. It did not gradually fade away or devolve into something else; it just stopped. Now, to be sure, there were complex reasons, both cultural and ecclesial, for this development. There was the general mistrust of institutions and authorities characteristic of the sixties, as well as the sexual revolution that sought to overthrow Victorian sexual mores and to liberate people for self-expression. And on the ecclesial front, there was a surely legitimate sense that confessional practice had become corrupt through an excessive legalism and ritualism — not to mention an overconcentration on the sins of the flesh.

But when, for whatever reasons, confession was dropped, it was, in accordance with Greeley's law, picked up all over the popular culture. Even a casual survey of daytime television reveals that the airwaves have become one giant and very public confessional box. On talk shows from Oprah, to Sally Jessy Raphael, to Jerry Springer, to Queen Latifah, people pour out their psychological tensions, sexual frustrations, family crises, and feelings of inadequacy, desperately hoping to find guidance, or at the very least, cathartic release. The problem, of course, is that this confession takes place, not in the context and according to the discipline of the Gospel, but in the presence of self-appointed TV gurus, pop psychologists, and audiences eager for thrills and sexual titillation. In a much more positive way, the lost confessional practice of examining one's conscience has been adopted by the twelve-step programs and their call for a "searching moral inventory." And above all, as is apparent everywhere around us, confession has transmuted into the practice of psychotherapy. Alasdair MacIntyre has argued that every culture holds up certain archetypes of human flourishing, embodiments of what it takes to be virtuous. Thus, the ancient Greek world privileged the soldier and the statesman, while the Renaissance lionized the artist and the businessman. The two roles that MacIntyre feels are singled out in our postmodern society are the manager (the one who tames tangled bureaucracies) and the therapist (the one who tames tangled psyches).[44] So what used to be whispered to one's confessor — guilt, anxiety, imperfection — is now spoken to a contemporary hero, one's therapist.

Now all of these more secular practices have their place (I suppose I could even include TV talk shows, if only for their entertainment value), but they are no substitutes for the ecclesial practice of confessing one's sins, in the style of Peter, Isaiah, and Paul. I believe that the church must reclaim this exercise unapologetically. Not to confess one's sins and to seek the forgiveness of God is to put oneself in mortal danger — and this statement is made, not in a legalistic tone, but a spiritual one. The breakdown in confessional practice has made the church sick by neglect.

The condition for the possibility of confession is an honest and thoroughgoing examination of conscience. As part of his Spiritual Exercises, Ignatius of Loyola recommends a frequent "consciousness examen," whereby one isolates a particular fault or sin and then carefully monitors how many times one has indulged in that behavior during a specified period of time.[45] The abuse of this practice, of course, is a sort of obsessive-compulsive focusing on misdeeds, but, when it is exercised prudently, it becomes an effective tool of honest introspection. At the outset of each eucharistic liturgy, the church encourages those who approach the sacred mysteries first to call to mind their sins and seek the divine mercy. This is the liturgical instantiation of Peter's "Lord, leave me for I am a sinful man," the awareness of imperfection that comes from proximity to the light.

At the end of his monastic journal, *The Sign of Jonas,* Thomas Merton inserts an epilogue called "Fire Watch: July 4th 1952." Jacques Maritain referred to this text as the most powerful piece of spiritual writing in the twentieth century. It is, on the surface of the narrative, an account of Merton's performance of one of the routine duties of a Gethsemani monk: walking through the monastery by night and stopping at various stations to check for fires. But on the symbolic level, it is a rather Dantesque metaphor of the process and practice of inner examination, the slumbering monastery representing Merton's own soul.

Merton sets out, once his brother monks are asleep, flashlight in hand and sneakers on his feet. The flashlight represents the light of awareness that he will shine into all corners of his life, and the sneakers the silence of his inner listening. He commences the fire watch in the deepest part of the monastery, on the ground level, where "your feet are walking on a floor of earth" and where "naked wires are exposed," and "it stinks of the hides of slaughtered calves."[46] This is the deepest and most elemental part of the soul, where one comes into direct contact with nature and with the animal instincts, and where the "hard-wiring" of the mind is plainly evident. On his way to the next station, Merton comes to a vat under which he once "burned letters that were in the pigeon holes of Father Abbot's room" and he spies a furnace where he "burned the rest of the papers he told me to burn."[47] This is, of course, the burning away that has to take place in the spiritual life. As we

journey around within, we find feelings, aspirations, thoughts, fears
that simply must be purged if the soul is to survive.

Next, our pilgrim comes to "the furnace room, the hottest station," and his language takes on an explicitly Dantean resonance:
"You fight your way through a jungle of wet clothes, drying in the
heat, and go down by the flanks of the boiler to the third station."[48]
At the pit of Hell, Dante and Virgil were forced to climb down the
"shaggy flanks" of Satan in order to make their way out. Here Merton confronts that which is most hellish in his soul, the place of
greatest confusion and sin — and, as always, he must investigate
and shine his flashlight. As he completes this stage of his itinerary,
he suddenly sees a vivid depiction of Christ, "the Holy Face," as
the tennis ball of his flashlight dances on the wall. It is precisely in
these lowest and most frightening places of the soul that we have
been accompanied by the Son of God.

Having gone all the way down, he now commences the journey upward. Coming to the choir novitiate, he confronts his own
personal past, as he is flooded by a wave of memories from years
before: "I am suddenly haunted by my first days in religion." Here
is the searching out of one's motivations, desires, decisions, mistakes, and life choices, a cleansing and exploration of the memory.
He then passes through the library, evocative of the mind, with
all of its ideas, arguments, and insights. He makes a special effort
to explore "Hell," that section of the monastic library containing
forbidden books. The point is clear: the whole of the mind must be
examined, even the most vile and dangerous of our ideas. After the
library, he comes to "the longest room in Kentucky," the dormitory
where the monks lie sleeping and dreaming. Just as the instincts,
the feelings, and the mind have to be investigated, so the realm of
the unconscious (for which Merton developed an acute sensitivity
in the latter part of his life) must be illuminated.

And finally, having crept through the whole of the place, Merton comes to the tower, the "pathway that leads up to the stars."
He notes that the staircase is an old one, "going back before the
Civil War" and therefore perilous: "You have to watch that third
step or your feet go through the boards."[49] This is the aspect of

Merton's soul that is explicitly and formally spiritual, that which opens on to the mystery of God. To climb around in this section of the psyche is, he knows, dangerous business, and he has to watch his step. When he gets to the top, he revels in the teeming life in the forest below and in the "frozen distance of the stars." And then he rests: "I lay the clock on the belfry ledge and prayed cross-legged with my back against the tower." Having made the night journey through all of the levels of his soul, having shone the light and asked the questions, he is now ready for the world around him; he is ready for mission. He concludes: "the fire watch is an examination of conscience in which your task as watchman suddenly appears in its true light: a pretext devised by God to isolate you and to search your soul with lamps and questions in the heart of darkness."[50]

Merton's beautifully crafted narrative is meant to evoke the practice that I am insisting upon: the searching out of one's life — carefully, prayerfully, painfully — in preparation for the confession of sin. Without this exercise, we remain caught by our hidden fault, tripped up and betrayed by it — and thus we are unfit for the third path of holiness.

Truth-Telling

Christians are people dedicated to living in the truth, because Jesus described himself as the Truth (John 14:6). We who worship Jesus cannot live in falsehood, because he is the criterion by which true and false are discriminated, the light in which the difference between good and evil is seen. Those who wish to live in the shadows must marginalize him, as Pilate did rhetorically — "What is Truth?" (John 18:38) — and as his own townspeople did more directly: "They led him to the brow of the hill on which their town was built, so that they might hurl him off the cliff" (Luke 4:29). But if we accept him as Messiah and Son of God, we must live the truth that he is, even when it costs us.

A key aspect of the peace treaty that emerged after the wars of religion and that helped to define modernity was a sweeping tolerance with regard to moral and metaphysical viewpoints.[51]

Because Europeans of the seventeenth and eighteenth centuries were not able to adjudicate such questions without violence, it was deemed wiser simply to accept a wide variety of opinions on ultimate matters, and this agreement has been largely accepted in the modern (and postmodern) West. What this has led to, of course, is a suspension of conflict (at least in some cases) but also a bland relativism, or even indifferentism, in regard to the most compelling and interesting questions that face us. In the social theories of Rawls and Habermas, we find the modern peace treaty vividly on display. In order to secure real justice for all, Rawls argues, the participants in a society must operate behind a "veil of ignorance," setting aside their personal convictions, preferences, and commitments. Thus they produce, at least in theory, a community without prejudice in favor of any particular person or group. Of course, in the process, they also produce an utterly beige society, void of those very depth-level commitments that make human life interesting and rich.[52] And Habermas holds that the good and just community is tantamount to a place where the dynamics of effective, open communication are fostered and respected. In his ideal scenario, the many representatives of a pluralistic society are assembled around the table of democratic conversation, and persuasive argument based solely upon a generally accessible reason is the guiding method.[53] The problem here is that the voices of those who hold convictions through faith (and who do not therefore accept the canons of reasonableness proposed by Habermas) are systematically excluded from the conversation. The assumption behind both theories is the typically modern one that religious commitments are essentially unjust and violent and must, accordingly, be marginalized.

In the film *The Contender*, this modern hostility to religion is, refreshingly, out in the open. One of the characters comments to another: "Church and state were separated in this country, not to protect religion from the state, but to protect the state from religion." But nowhere is the peace treaty more radically expressed than in the extraordinary *Casey* decision of the United States Supreme Court in regard to abortion. Carrying the modern setting-aside of religious and metaphysical truth to its logical extreme, the justices commented: "At the heart of liberty is the right to define one's own concept of existence, of meaning, of the universe, of the mystery of human life."[54] In the interests of holding together a pluralist society, the justices leave the determination of the deepest and most important questions wholly to the whim of individuals, freedom having completely trumped truth.

But Christians can have no truck with this form of liberalism, for we do not think that Christ's truth can be bracketed or set aside for the purposes of an ersatz peace. In fact, we sniff out behind the rhetoric of inclusion and tolerance a rather fierce violence against religion in general and Christianity in particular. Rather, we are convinced that authentic peace and liberty will be achieved only in correlation to the Word of God which appropriately grounds them. Paul can say, "It is for freedom that Christ set you free," and he can proclaim himself "a slave of Christ Jesus" (Rom. 1:1), because he is not saddled with a modern conception of freedom. He knows that when we are enslaved to the truth that appeared in Christ, we are free to realize who God wants us to be. Pope John Paul II stands in this Pauline tradition when he insists, in *Veritatis Splendor*, that freedom and truth must always be yoked together, lest freedom lapse into arbitrariness and truth devolve into oppression.

Hence, a key practice of the Christian church is the telling of the truth, even when it hurts. Stanley Hauerwas reminds us that one of the first pastoral interventions described in the Acts of the Apostles is a truth-telling that shames two people right into their graves.[55] So much for the Christian minister as one-sidedly kind and gentle! And it is surely significant that the entire coterie of Jesus' apostles (John excepted) died martyrs' deaths. Disciplining one's speech in the interests of getting along did not seem to be, for them, a high priority. Can we read that terrible and wonderful book of martyrs, the Apocalypse of John, without seeing the power of bold, truthful proclamation in the early Christian church? And the cloud of witnesses grows up and down the Christian centuries, taking in a huge number in the century just concluded: Padre Pro shouting "Viva el Cristo Rey" to his executioners; Franz Jaggerstätter and Dietrich Bonhoeffer challenging to their dying breaths the lies of Nazism; Dorothy Day enduring taunts, imprisonment, and marginalization because she spoke of Christ's nonviolent love in the midst of a war-loving society; Martin Luther King taking an assassin's bullet because he insisted on being a drum major for New Testament justice.

And in the last decades of the twentieth century, Christian truth-telling was, once again, dangerously at work. Václav Havel, the president of the Czech Republic and one-time dissident playwright, commented on the role that he and his fellow writers played during the dark years of communist domination in eastern Europe during the 1970s. In a society dominated by lies, they decided simply to tell the truth. They knew that Communism thrived on untruths concerning God, human nature, and social structures, and they realized, furthermore, that the tissue of deception held together only because of the constant threat of arrest or, in direst circumstances, military intervention. Like the guileless child in the tale of the emperor's new clothes, Havel and his companions resolved not to cooperate with an illusion supported by fear. For their troubles they were, of course, arrested and persecuted, but through their speaking and writing they, in Havel's words, "cleared out a space for the truth."[56] And into that space people came and found they were able to move; and soon, more joined them, then more and more — until the society of lies was no longer able to sustain itself.

Something very similar happened in Poland during the 1980s. When John Paul II arrived in his homeland for his first visit as pope in 1979, his countrymen came out by the millions to hear him, despite numerous obstacles — physical and psychological — thrown up by the communist regime. In a remarkably prescient editorial, Jimmy Carter's National Security Advisor, Zbigniew Brzezinski, said that, in the wake of that visit, communism in Poland was finished. This was before the formation of the Solidarity trade union and a full decade before the actual fall of the Soviet-backed regime. But what Brzezinski saw was millions and millions of people moving into a space of truth that the pope, by his words and presence, opened up. In the face of that, the illusion simply could not be maintained, no matter how many tanks and bombs defended it. And the forced dispelling of the illusion is precisely what took place throughout the eighties in Poland, aided and abetted at key moments by a pope who wasn't afraid to speak the truth about God and humanity.

What I hope these last few paragraphs have made clear is that Christian truth-telling in the twentieth century has challenged both of the great ideological options of the modern era. Both liberalism (by bracketing the truth in the name of freedom) and communism (by distorting it in the name of justice) have become the enemies of Christ's truthful church. And this is why both have tried — the first more subtly and the second more brutally — to silence that dangerous community.

Now having seen the necessity of prophetic speech in the Christian church, what can we say about the rules that ought to govern and limit that speech? Because the central message of Jesus is compassion, because the Lord names sin clearly and then reaches out in love, the discipline of Christian truth-telling must be this: even true speech, offered in a spirit of retribution and hatred, is to be avoided because it undermines itself, becoming spiritually false in the very act of utterance. Or to state it more positively: Christian speech is true, not only to its object, but to itself only when it is realized in love. John Shea formulated a principle in this regard that is as helpful as it is difficult: criticize someone precisely in the measure that you are willing to help that person deal with the problem that you have raised. If your commitment to help is nil, you should remain silent; if your willingness to help is moderate, your critique should be moderate; if you are willing to do all in your power to address the situation with the person, speak the whole truth. This is not unrelated to Aquinas's point about relating anger to justice: one could be perfectly right in one's criticism, but morally wrong if that critique is not made in the real desire to ameliorate the problem.

Another extremely helpful guide to the practice of truth-telling is found in Matthew 18, where we find a sort of moral application of the principle of subsidiarity. Jesus is instructing his community in the difficult task of correcting an errant brother or sister: "If another member of the church sins against you, go and point out the fault when the two of you are alone. If the member listens to you, you have regained that one" (Matt. 18:15). Avoid the practice of gossiping and complaining to others about a grievance; rather, confront the person who has offended you directly and courageously. That way, the difficulty is addressed, the loving concern of the complainant is evident, and the process of rumor, attack, counterattack, innuendo, and scapegoating is arrested. Now, if the person does not respond to this loving intervention, "take one or two others along with you, so that every word may be confirmed by the evidence of two or three witnesses" (Matt. 18:16). Thus, the wider community is involved, but only minimally — enough to bring the offender to repentance. Only if this small circle of the church is ignored should one bring the complaint to the whole community. What is so rich here is the pursuit of the issue (since speaking the truth, even when it is dangerous, is essential), coupled with a deep care for the person in question and also for the entire family of the church (since love is our constant call). And then the wonderful conclusion: "and if the offender refuses to listen even to the church, let such a one be to you as a Gentile and a tax collector" (Matt. 18:17). This sounds, at first, like a total rejection, but then we recall how Jesus treated the Gentiles and tax collectors — eating with them, pursuing them, drawing them into the circle. There might be a moment of rejection and expulsion in the process of fraternal correction (as we can see, for example, in the Pauline epistles), but it is only provisional and only for the sake of eventual reconciliation.

St. Augustine, who was never afraid to speak the hard truth when necessary, followed the recommendations of Matthew 18 very concretely. Over the table in his episcopal residence where he dined with the priests of his diocese hung a sign that read: "If you speak ill of your brother here, you are not welcome at this table." And it is said that the bishop of Hippo would enforce the rule, pointing to the sign when one of his charges began complaining or gossiping.

Forgiveness

Forgiveness is one of the most vital and most misunderstood practices on path two. Its importance should be obvious from the Gospels themselves where it is centrally featured in both the preaching and praxis of Jesus. The forgiveness even of enemies is insisted upon in the Sermon on the Mount, and the pardoning of those who trespass against us is at the heart of the prayer that Jesus taught his church. But more to the point, Jesus' own startling practice of forgiving the sins of others emerges as one of the distinctive and most controversial elements in his ministry: "Why does this fellow speak this way? Who can forgive sins but God alone?" (Mark 2:7). And both rhetoric and practice reach their fullest expression when the crucified Jesus asks the Father to forgive those who are torturing him to death and when the risen Jesus says "Shalom" to those who have abandoned him. We speak the truth because Jesus is the Truth; we forgive because he forgave.

But what exactly is forgiveness? We must not, despite our typically modern tendency to do so, subjectivize and interiorize forgiveness, as though it amounted to little more than a conviction or a resolution. To say, "I have put that offense out of my mind and have resolved to move on" is not forgiveness; even to feel no further anger at someone who has hurt me and to refrain from harming that person is not tantamount to real forgiveness. Forgiveness, in the full New Testament sense of the term, is an act and not an attitude. It is the active and embodied repairing of a broken relationship, even in the face of opposition, violence, or indifference. When a relationship is severed, each party should, in justice, do his part to reestablish the bond. Forgiveness — which of necessity transcends justice — is the bearing of the other person's burden, moving toward her, even when she refuses to move an inch toward you. There is something relentless, even aggressive, about forgiveness, since it amounts to a refusal ever to give up on a relationship. "Lord, how many times should I forgive my brother?

Seven times?" Simon Peter asks Jesus; comes the reply: "I assure you, not seven times, but seventy times seven times." Christians should never cease in our efforts to establish love.

Stanley Hauerwas relates a terrible story of authentic forgiveness. There was an Amish family — a father, a mother, and their teenaged son — riding along, as was their custom, in a horse-drawn buggy. Behind them came a car filled with rowdy and impatient young people. Annoyed at the slow-moving carriage, they honked the horn and waved their fists in aggravation. Finally, in a swirl of dust, they rushed around the Amish. As they passed, one of the young men in the car hurled a stone in the direction of the horse, hoping just to harass the family. Instead, the stone hit the Amish boy in the head, killing him instantly. The town was outraged, and the young killer came to trial for manslaughter. To everyone's amazement, the parents of the slain teenager, still crippled by grief, appeared to testify on behalf of the stone-thrower. Despite this testimony, the young man was condemned and sent to prison. Now, every month, the Amish parents come to the jail and visit their son's slayer, comforting him, encouraging him, seeking to bring him back eventually into the community. That is forgiveness.

A similar story unfolded in Chicago in 1995. Cardinal Joseph Bernardin was accused of having sexually abused a young man, Steven Cook, years before, when Cook was a seminarian and the cardinal was archbishop of Cincinnati. When the story became public, the cardinal appeared before dozens of cameras and hundreds of reporters at a wrenching news conference. As his image and the terrible charge were transmitted all over the world, he had to endure the most humiliating and intrusive questions, under the literally glaring light of publicity. In the ensuing weeks, he endured a sort of Garden of Gethsemane. Following his usual busy public schedule, he would appear at Masses, gatherings, and social events, and, as the people turned to face him, he knew, to his infinite shame, that many of them probably believed the charge against him. During that period, the cardinal came to Mundelein Seminary where I teach, and he addressed the seminarians. He told them that when he prayed, he now stretched himself out full on the floor and begged God to take this suffering from him.

Eventually Steven Cook admitted that his accusations were groundless, and the charges were withdrawn. At this point, who would have blamed Cardinal Bernardin if he had lashed out in anger, condemning Cook and the media, perhaps threatening to countersue? And wouldn't we have praised him if he had quietly said, "Well, I am going to let this go and move on"? But he did neither of these things; instead, he chose to forgive. He visited Steven Cook in his home, embraced him, celebrated Mass with him, gave him a gift of the Bible, anointed him, and prayed with him. Bernardin bore absolutely no responsibility for the severed relationship between himself and Cook; it was brought about exclusively through the efforts of his accuser. In strict justice, therefore, he was obliged to do nothing to repair it. But, as the Scripture says, "mercy mocks justice." Bearing his accuser's burden, the cardinal made the overture that the young man was unable to make — and in doing that, he forgave.

Why do I relate this radical practice to the second path of holiness? To walk the second path is to know that we are sinners and that we, accordingly, stand in constant need of forgiveness. What makes our forgiveness of others necessary is their sin; but what makes it possible is our deep gratitude for having been first forgiven ourselves. This becomes clear in the Gospel story of the penitent prostitute in the house of Simon the Pharisee. To the shock of the gathered company, a woman of ill-repute approaches the rabbi from Nazareth, weeping onto his feet and anointing them with oil. Furious at the woman and disappointed in the altogether too permissive rabbi, Simon reacts violently: "If this man were a prophet, he would have know who and what kind of woman this is who is touching him — that she is a sinner" (Luke 7:39). But Jesus gently corrects his host: "I entered your house; you gave me no water for my feet, but she has bathed my feet with her tears and dried them with her hair. You gave me no kiss, but from the time I came in she has not stopped kissing my feet.... Therefore, I tell you, her sins, which were many, have been forgiven; hence she has shown great love" (Luke 7:44–47). Simon is so spiritually cramped, so unable to love, because he has not yet felt the power of being forgiven; the woman overflows with love because she has felt to the bottom of her soul that her many sins have been wiped away. As Paul Tillich pointed out in his sermon on this passage, it is not that she loves and is therefore forgiven; rather, it is that she is forgiven and therefore loves.

In accordance with the governing intuition of path two, when we know that we are forgiven sinners, we become agents of divine forgiveness in the world, grateful bearers of others' burdens, bold speakers of the hard truth.

Chapter Three

Walking the Third Path: Realizing Your Life Is Not about You

None of us lives as his own master;
none of us dies as his own master....
Both in life and death, we are the Lord's.
—Rom. 14:7–8

I am hanging in the balance
of a perfect, finished plan.
Like every sparrow fallen
Like every grain of sand.
—Bob Dylan

All artists love what they give birth to — parents love their chil-
dren; poets love their poems; craftsmen love their handiwork. How
then could God hate a single thing since God is the artist of
everything? —Thomas Aquinas

At the end of John's Gospel, the risen Jesus speaks with Peter. "When you were a young man, you used to fasten your own belt and to go wherever you wished. But when you grow old, you will stretch out your hands, and someone else will fasten a belt around you and take you where you do not wish to go" (John 21:18).

In the initiation rites of many primal peoples, an adolescent boy would be kidnapped from his home by a band of men, including his own father. He would be scarified in some way — a tooth knocked out or a cheek cut — and then he would be introduced into the lore and history of his tribe. Finally, he would be brought to the edge of forest or jungle, given a few provisions, and told to fend for himself until he was visited by his spirit guide. Only then, having been forced out of his self-regarding egotism and brought into the wider worlds of tribe, nature, and the Spirit, would he be allowed to take his place in the community.

Only when we realize that our lives are situated in a context of a Life that stretches infinitely beyond them, only when we know that our wills are related to a Will that encompasses and surpasses the whole of the cosmos, are we ready to live. Paul closes the third chapter of his letter to the Ephesians with this prayer: "Now to him who by the power at work within us is able to accomplish abundantly more than all we can ask or imagine, to him be glory in the church and in Christ Jesus" (Eph. 3:20–21). And Matthew brings his Gospel to completion with Jesus' great commission: "Go therefore and make disciples of all the nations.... And remember I am with you always, to the end of the age" (Matt. 28:19–20). This is the third path of holiness: coming to terms with the fact that our lives are not about us. There is Another who will tie us up and take us where we never imagined we could or would go; there is a Power that is operative in us and accompanies us whether we know it or not and that will accomplish what we, by our own power, could never accomplish. To allow ourselves to be tied up and taken, to surrender to the greater authority, is to walk the third and most dramatic of the ways of holiness. On the first path, we are drawn close to Christ the center; on the second path, we are healed and transformed, all the energies of our souls finding their ground and direction in Christ; then, on the third path, we are sent to do the work of Jesus, perhaps even to "accomplish greater things" than he himself (John 14:12).

We notice a common element in all of the illustrations of path three just offered: receptivity. The Power will not be coerced; it does the coercing. Earlier, we saw that the intellectual problem with Adam and Eve was the Promethean misunderstanding and that their consequent moral problem was the grasping at that which can only be accepted as a gift. Path three is the undoing of this sin of Eden. Adam and Eve became cramped and frightened *pusillae animae* (little souls) when they determined to exercise their wills in the presence of the Will; we become *magnae animae* (great souls) in the measure that we let the Will exercise itself in us.[1]

Daniel Barenboim, the classical pianist, John Coltrane, the jazz saxophonist, and Eric Clapton, the rock guitarist, all said the same thing: their best playing occurs when they are no longer playing the instrument, but it is playing them. All three of those figures were meticulously trained, all three had become "masters" of their respective instruments, but they realized that they produced the most beautiful sounds, only at the limit of their striving and accomplishing, when they let the music carry them away. There is something very similar at work in the spiritual dimension, a rhythm between achieving and being achieved, between breathing in and breathing out. Teilhard de Chardin expressed it as the distinction between divinizing one's activities and divinizing one's passivities.[2] We can and should seek the Lord in all of our actions and to the limits of our powers, but the richest participation in the divine life occurs only when we stop seeking and we allow God to elevate us.

There is a section of St. Anselm's *Proslogion* that almost no one reads. It is a short autobiographical reflection that sets the context for the famous "ontological argument" for God's existence. Most commentators rush past it to get to the controversial proof, but if it is overlooked, the proof itself becomes, in my view, unintelligible. Anselm tells us that he produced this work at the prompting of his brother monks, who were searching for a single elegant demonstration for God's existence.[3] Now, neither Anselm nor his brothers were academics — they were Benedictine monks who had given their lives over to the process of finding and being found by God. Thus, the curiosity of Anselm's brothers was not primarily intellectual but spiritual and experiential; they wanted access to the true God, not because they were scholars looking for clarity, but because they were like deer yearning for running streams. Unable to turn down this ardent request, Anselm went in search of the demonstration but found himself frustrated: "Although I often and earnestly directed my thought to this end, and at some times that which I sought seemed to be just within my reach, while again it wholly evaded my mental vision, at last in despair I was about to cease, as if from the search for a thing which could not be found."[4] One of the most acute and powerful minds of the Middle Ages found himself blocked — as long as he looked.

In despair, Anselm decided to drive the thought from his mind, "busying himself to no purpose." But he found that, the more he tried to ignore it, the more "it began to force itself" on him with a sort of importunity, until one day, when he was worn out with the effort of resisting it, the proof of which he had despaired "offered itself," so that he "eagerly embraced the thoughts" which he had been "strenuously repelling." Precisely when he stopped looking, the insight that he was seeking found him. What came to him was the sacred name of God as "that than which no greater can be thought," and it should be obvious that this idea and the mode of its arrival are correlated. For the name he discovered is not any kind of description of God, still less a definition, but rather a principle or heuristic device: whatever you can name or think is less than God himself. God is that which, in principle, lies beyond or under all of your attempts to find him.

Now it is just this insight that is elaborated upon in the so-called ontological argument that follows. Anselm's conclusion from the sacred name is that the true God can be sequestered neither in the interiority of one's subjectivity, nor in the sheer objectivity of the outside world, but must transcend or lie beneath that distinction. That than which no greater can be thought is neither "in here," nor "out there," because beings in such dimensions could be rather easily thought. Whatever God is, he is not to be caught in the net of concepts, ideas, or images; whatever he is must, in principle, be received as a gift. This is why the "argument" of Anselm is really a description of the Christian life on the third path of holiness: we experience the truth of God when we surrender our minds to him and give up our pathetic attempts to control him.[5]

The Church Fathers were fond of exploring the relationship between Eve, mother of all the living, and the new Eve, Mary the Mother of God. Where Eve grasped and lost, Mary surrendered and received; where Eve said no to the alluring mystery, Mary said yes. The angel of the Lord — an agent from a realm beyond what can be seen and known — appears to the maid of Nazareth and greets her in what Balthasar describes as the language of heaven: "Hail, full of grace." The sinful earth is a place of grasping, but the angel salutes her as someone who is ready to accept gifts. Then he lays out for her the divine plan in which she is to play a signal role: "And now you will conceive in your womb and bear a son, and you will name him Jesus. He will be great, and will be called the Son of the Most High" (Luke 1:32). Standing still within the confines of what she can know, Mary responds, "How can this be, since I am a virgin?" What the angel has told her does not conform to her expectations, and she is, understandably enough, puzzled. Then the messenger speaks the language of path three: "The Holy Spirit will come upon you, and the power of the Most High will overshadow you" (Luke 1:35). In other words: someone much more powerful than you will overwhelm your physical, moral, intellectual, and spiritual capacities, and in the measure that you cooperate with this intervention, you will come to a life you hadn't imagined. Finally, he reminds Mary of her cousin Elizabeth's unlikely pregnancy and adds, "nothing will be impossible for God" (Luke 1:37).

Søren Kierkegaard, tweaking the noses of the tidy rationalists of his day, said that authentic faith is a "passion for the impossible." It is a surrender in love to that which the mind (the too-often arrogant determiner of what is and is not possible) cannot see. When Mary says, "Here am I, the servant of the Lord; let it be with me according to your word," she exhibits such faith and thereby undoes the refusal of Eve. And this *fiat* to the impossible made possible the Incarnation of God. In accepting the seduction of the alluring Mystery, she allowed God's love to become enfleshed for the transformation of the world. In the Catholic faith, Mary is praised as the mother of the church, the matrix of all discipleship. What this means is that her *fiat* is the ground and model of every disciple's response to God's desire for incarnation. Meister Eckhart said that all believers become "mothers of Christ," bearers of the incarnate word, in the measure that they acquiesce to the divine passion to push concretely into creation.[6]

Mission

Thus, your life is not about you, in a general sense, because it is related to the infinite mystery of God, but in a more pointed sense, because it is always about God's missionary purposes. The neo-Platonist philosopher Plotinus summed up the spiritual life in the phrase: to be alone with the Alone. Plotinian devotees would certainly agree that their lives are not about them, but they would have no sense of being *sent* anywhere by the Alone. There is not the slightest trace of this self-absorbed mysticism in the biblical tradition. No one in the Bible is ever given an experience of God without being sent on mission to do the work of God. Abraham hears the call and is then told to go to a distant land (Gen. 12:1–2); Moses sees the burning bush and then is commissioned to liberate his people (Exod. 3:4–12); Isaiah sees the display of God's glory in the temple and says "Here I am; send me" (Isa. 6:1–8); Saul is blinded by the light of Jesus' presence and appointed a missionary to the Gentiles (Acts 9:3–19). The biblical rule seems to be: first you see, then you go.

In *The Soul's Code,* James Hillman revives the ancient mythological idea that all of us are born with the seeds of who we are destined to become planted within us. The success or failure of one's life is measured according to the development or frustration of these seeds. He calls this the "acorn theory." Thus, for example, the young Yehudi Menuhin was taken to a violin concert by his father. Immediately the acorn was stirred, and he knew that playing that instrument was his vocation and so asked his father to get him a violin. Amused at the boy's intensity and insistence, the father bought him a toy instrument. Infuriated, the young Menuhin grabbed the toy and hurled it against the wall, smashing it to pieces. His father then bought him a violin. Or the young Ella Fitzgerald was slated to dance at a local talent show. When she was intro-duced and stood before the audience, the acorn was stirred and she decided, on the spot, to forgo her dance routine and she sang, to the delight of the surprised crowd. Both performers realized their callings, and there was no room for negotiation or compromise.

The Christian tradition says that we are all created "through Christ." This means that, at the very root of our being, from our "beginning," we are meant to realize a Christomorphic destiny, playing out, in a unique manner, the form of Jesus. Like Hillman's "acorn," this *imago* is in us, whether we like it or not, and the drama of our lives is nothing but the discovery and unfolding of it. Jesus speaks of the treasure buried in a field that a man stumbles upon. And when he finds it, he sells everything he has in order to buy that field (Matt. 13:44–46). Could the field be the human heart, the treasure be the *imago* of Christ, and could the selling of everything be the surrendering of all for the sake of the mission? And he speaks of the merchant's search for a pearl of great price; when the pearl is found, the merchant sells everything in order to acquire it. Could this pearl be his Christoform identity, the one thing worth looking for? And could the selling off of everything else be living out of the successful, centered life? Joseph Campbell says that the greatest tragedy in life is not so much failure, but rather climbing the ladder of success and finding out that it is up against the wrong wall! Bob Dylan was reflecting ruefully on the same phenomenon when he said, "You find out when you reach the top / you're on the bottom."[7] We can spend our entire life in pursuit of goals that are worthless, or even goals that are objectively good but not *ours*, or better, Christ's for us.

The second section of Hans Urs von Balthasar's great theologi-cal triptych is called *Theodramatik* (Theo-drama).[8] The assumption that governs this work is that God is the director and writer of a drama that involves the whole of creation, but especially the char-acters who are his rational creatures. What God wants is that each of us finds our role in the drama that God is concocting. The tragedy of sin is nothing but the preference for the ego-drama over the theo-drama, insisting that I play the starring role (of course) in the play that I am writing and directing. In that case, my desires, my goals, and my style are paramount. But in the context of the theo-drama, all of that is turned around: now it is God's desire for me, God's goal for me, God's style played out in me that matter. The particular roles within the theo-drama are as varied as the actors, but their purpose is always the same, because God's drama has one end: to join others to the power of the divine life. In the *Paradiso*, the final section of Dante's *Divine Comedy*, the angels fly back and forth from the divine source, much as bees fly to and from a flower, carrying the longings of earth to heaven and the peace of heaven to earth.[9] That is an icon of the theo-drama.

As Balthasar spells out the implications of the divine drama, he isolates three basic types or forms of Christian discipleship, corresponding to the constellation of three apostles who gathered intimately around Jesus: Peter, John, and Paul.[10] The mission of every baptized person will conform to one of these three basic patterns. Peter embodies and symbolizes the role of office in the church of Christ. His presence in the Gospels and the Acts of the Apostles is unavoidable — he is a key player in all five of those texts — and his role is clear: he is leader, spokesman, orderer of the charisms. The body of Christ requires leadership and authority because it has work to do: the Christification of the world. Those who share in the Petrine ministry order, direct, guide, and coordinate the myriad powers that are available in the body in order to facilitate this task. Over the centuries this mission has been carried out by bishops, popes, priests, ministers, elders, directors, and administrators. What emerges with great clarity in the Peter stories of the New Testament is that this office requires courage and a profound willingness to suffer. Jesus must rebuke Peter directly when he shrinks from the demands of the cross ("Get behind me, Satan!" (Mark 8:33), and the Lord explicitly tells the head of the apostles on the night before he suffered: "Simon, Simon, listen! Satan has demanded to sift all of you like wheat, but I have prayed for you that your own faith may not fail" (Luke 22:31–32). This suffering and discipline is required precisely because tyranny, the shadow side of this kingly office, is, as John Henry Newman knew, always a danger. Leaders within the church can begin to order the charisms, not for the good of the body, but for the aggrandizement of their own egos, and this abuse leads the community by a short road to disaster.

John symbolizes another basic form of Christian life. He was the beloved disciple, the one who laid his head on the breast of Jesus at the Last Supper. Accordingly, he embodies the mystical, contemplative, liturgical aspect of the church, those disciples who listen intently to the heart of the Lord. These are not the order-ers of the many charisms; rather, they are those who, in love with Jesus, worship and watch. In the account of the empty tomb in the Gospel of John, it is the beloved disciple who races ahead of Peter and arrives at the tomb first. He looks in and believes. And in that same Gospel's telling of the postresurrection appearance by the Sea of Galilee, it is once again John who sees before the others: "It is the Lord!" (John 21:7). Only upon hearing this Jo-hannine cry does Peter jump into the water and swim to Jesus. These stories evoke the mystical intuition that "sees" before office, and more clearly. Whenever the church of Jesus "royally wastes its time,"[11] contemplating, listening, savoring, praying, the Johannine type is in the ascendency. The missions of artists, poets, architects, dramatists, liturgists, mystics, and spiritual masters correspond to this archetype of Christian discipleship. In Newman's language, these are the fulfillers of the "priestly" office. Their role is indis-pensable, but, like the Petrine role, it carries a shadow, in this case superstition or irrational enthusiasm, believing, if you will, too much.

Paul is the representative of Balthasar's third archetype of the Christian life. Not so much organizer or mystic, Paul was a preacher, proclaimer, and, in the ordinary sense of the word, missionary. In the face of enormous obstacles — psychologi-cal, institutional, and physical — Paul *went out* and spoke the Word. Restless, unsatisfied, feisty, intellectually curious, he is the prototype of all Christian philosophers, theologians, teachers, adventurers, and missionaries — those who, in different ways, would engage the culture around them. Augustine of Canterbury, Francis Xavier, Thomas Aquinas, Martin Luther, John Wesley, and Billy Graham would thus all be Pauline Christians. Newman characterized this type under the heading of "prophet," speaker of the truth. And he noticed its shadow as a cold rationalism, a tendency, perhaps born from too much intercourse with a non-Christian culture, to believe too little.

For both Balthasar and Newman, the health of the body of Christ depends upon a creative and tensive balance among these three forms of mission. When the Petrine dominates, the Pauline and Johannine are tyrannized and the essential life of the church is compromised; when the Johannine dominates, the community can fall into a sort of self-regarding torpor or self-undermining anti-intellectualism; when the Pauline dominates, the church can lose its soul and direction. The *desideratum* is a vibrant exercise of all three. One of the tragedies in ecclesial life is that someone who is meant to fulfill one type of mission erroneously chooses another, out of either ignorance or ambition or fear. Thus, the born mystic is pushed by pride to become an orderer of charisms, or the one destined to be a prophet is seduced into a liturgical/contemplative life. In such cases, it is not only the person in question who suffers; it is the entire body of the church. (Hans Urs von Balthasar himself was twice offered the cardinal's hat by Pope John Paul II, and twice he refused, insisting that he, a natural Johannine, was not destined to share in the Petrine or governing ministry. After the third invitation, he very reluctantly accepted, out of respect for the pope's wishes, but then, fittingly enough, died just days before the ceremony of conferral!) This is why Balthasar places underneath all three forms of mission, as a matrix, the Marian mission.[12] Mary said yes to the angel, even when she had no clear idea what accepting that invitation meant. Placing her own desires aside, she agreed to be an agent of the divine Desire. Accordingly, Petrines, Paulines, and Johannines must all be Marians if they are to be of service to the body of Christ. They must all acquiesce to the divine purposes, realizing that their lives are not about them.

I wonder whether the tragic divisions in the body of Jesus are, at least to some degree, the result of the separating out of these missions. To speak very broadly, the Roman Catholic branch of Christianity (in its hierarchy and papacy) placed a great stress on the Petrine office, whereas the Protestant branch (in its embrace of Scripture and proclamation) emphasized the Pauline, and the Orthodox branch (in its strong liturgical focus) favored the Johannine. The work of the church will be carried out most effectively only when these three streams join again in one river.

A Flannery O'Connor Interlude

We have already seen how Flannery O'Connor illuminated the second path of holiness in her account of the conversion of Mrs. Turpin, but I turn to her again because her novel *The Violent Bear It Away* is an irresistibly powerful narrative display of the third path. One of only two novels that O'Connor ever wrote, this text is, like so many of her stories, shocking, convoluted in plot, funny, violent, and filled with unforgettably strange characters. It is also, from beginning to end, haunted by the Holy Spirit and his call to mission. To walk through the surprising story line of this novel, in the company of its bizarre players, is to feel viscerally what it means to know that your life is not about you.

The soul of the novel is Old Tarwater, a dirt farmer who is also a prophet of God. His absurdly complex, gothic story is told in flashback, as the novel opens, in typical Flannery O'Connor style, with a macabre account of his death and burial: "Francis Marion Tarwater's uncle had been dead for only half a day when the boy got too drunk to finish digging his grave and a Negro named Buford Munson... had to finish it and drag the body from the breakfast table where it was still sitting and bury it in a decent and Christian way."[13] After recovering from that opening sentence, we learn, bit by bit, as the narrative unfolds, the contours of his biography. When his sister had given birth to a son, Rayber, the old man had kidnapped the child because he was convinced that he would be raised in an unhealthy spiritual environment. For several years, he had the boy and trained him in the life of a prophet. In time, the boy's stepfather came through the woods and claimed him, not with enthusiasm but out of legal obligation, and, reluctantly, the old prophet let him go. Now Rayber came of age, trained in the ways of the modern world, far from the influence of his uncle whom most considered mad. Many years later, Rayber's sister became pregnant out of wedlock and was then involved, along with her child's father, in a horrendous auto accident which killed the two of them. But just before passing away, the mother gave birth to a boy, who was then claimed by his uncle. Seeing his opportunity to redress the wrong of many years before and seized by a prophetic call, Old Tarwater kidnapped this child, his grand-nephew, and spirited him into the woods in order to rescue him from a godless upbringing. When Rayber returned to his own prophetic training ground to wrest the child from the grip of the old man, Tarwater took out a shotgun and wounded Rayber in the leg and the ear, sending him scampering back across the corn field.

Securely in possession of the child (now named young Tarwater), the old prophet began to educate him according to the Christian way, teaching him "Figures, Reading, Writing and History beginning with Adam expelled from the Garden and going on down through the presidents to Herbert Hoover and on in speculation toward the Second Coming and the Day of Judgment."[14] In short, Old Tarwater taught the young man to situate the many branches of human knowledge in the context of sacred history, thereby relating, as St. Bonaventure urged in the Middle Ages, truths to the Truth. He also schooled the young man in the ways of the prophet, telling him to expect the call of the Lord and to prepare himself for his mission. Most importantly, he told him of the evils that would necessarily befall one who is summoned by God, "those that come from the world, which are trifling, and those that come from the Lord and burn the prophet clean." He was mentoring young Tarwater by drawing the boy's story into the greater stories of God's suffering servants "Abel and Enoch, and Noah and Job, Abraham and Moses, King David and Solomon and all the prophets, from Elijah who escaped death, to John whose severed head struck ter-

ror from a dish."[15] And he concluded his training by telling him
what his first prophetic acts would be. First, when his mentor died,
the boy would be obliged to bury him deep enough so that the
dogs couldn't dig him up and to place the sign of the cross over
his grave. Then, he would have to go into the city and baptize the
retarded child who had been born to his uncle Rayber some years
after Old Tarwater had chased him off of his property. By these
two gestures, young Tarwater would commence his career as God's
spokesman.

With all of this in the background, the central narrative begins — as we saw, with Old Tarwater's death. When the old prophet
died across from him at the breakfast table, young Tarwater finished
his meal and then began to scrape a grave out of the ground. Under
the hot sun and wearied by the effort, the boy put down his shovel
and, rather willfully, got drunk. At this point, he engaged in a dialogue with an inner voice, identified as the "stranger." In one of
her letters, Flannery O'Connor did not hesitate to name this character, who consistently mocked the wishes of the old man, as the
devil. The stranger told the boy that Old Tarwater was crazy, or if
not simply crazy, at least the victim of an *idée fixe*: "he didn't have
but one thing on his mind. He was a one notion man. Jesus. Jesus
this and Jesus that. Ain't you ... fed up and sick to the roof of your
mouth with Jesus?" Turning more directly on the boy, the stranger
tells him that there is a stark choice in life, an either/or. "Jesus
or the devil," young Tarwater suggests. "No, no, no," the stranger
corrects him, "It ain't Jesus or the devil. It's Jesus or *you*."[16] In her
"A Good Man Is Hard to Find," O'Connor's murdering character,
the Misfit, states the same Kierkegaardian opposition: with regard
to Jesus, he says, "If He did what he said, then it's nothing for
you to do but throw away everything and follow Him, and if He
didn't, then it's nothing for you to do but enjoy the few minutes
you got left the best way you can."[17] Either your life is about Jesus
and his mission or it is about you. There is no third option. Young
Tarwater's wrestling with this choice drives the narrative of the rest
of the novel.

Though his great-uncle had always been sure of young Tarwater's prophetic vocation, the boy himself remained of divided mind. Throughout his childhood, he had looked for dramatic confirmation of God's call — a burning bush or an unambiguous heavenly manifestation — but had found none. Thus, at the moment of truth, when he was summoned to perform his first prophetic act, he balked and ran. Hours later, still in a drunken stupor and not realizing that a Negro neighbor had finished the task and buried the old man, young Tarwater, frustrated and angry, set fire to the house and headed off for town, encouraged by the promptings of the stranger. His destination was the home of his uncle Rayber, the rationalist failed prophet whom Old Tarwater had shot and whose "idiot child" was awaiting baptism. Thus, the boy fled directly onto the horns of his dilemma.

When Rayber met him at the door, the boy was shocked by his appearance. Because of his shotgun wound, he was unable to hear and so had outfitted himself with an elaborate hearing aid, involving a metal box near his belt and a series of wires that ran from there up through his glasses and into his injured ear. A robot, an artificial man, he emerges as an apt symbol of the modern consciousness that is able to take in only what is mediated through technology. But his uncle was delighted to see young Tarwater — this unfortunate soul now liberated from the insane world of the backwoods prophet — and he resolved to give him all of the advantages of a modern, rational education. In the voice of every Enlightenment philosopher he says, "Listen boy, getting out from under the old man is just like coming out of the darkness into the light." But at that moment, the white-haired, dim-witted child, named wonderfully enough "Bishop," shambled into the room and "stood there, dim and ancient, like a child who had been a child for centuries."[18] Hatred for prophecy and the call to prophecy, the either/or, faced the young man.

Filled with an eager enthusiasm to make up for lost time, Rayber began escorting young Tarwater all over town, to supermarkets, museums, the post office, the railroad yards, the city hall, hoping to introduce him to the universe the old man had shut out. The boy remained utterly uninterested until they came to a "large grimey garage-like structure," over the door of which hung a banner that read "Unless ye be born again ye shall not have everlasting life." This pentecostal tabernacle seized the boy's attention. Aware of the "sinister pull" such a place would have on young Tarwater, Rayber inquired in the tones of the sympathetic therapist, "Does this interest you, does it remind you of something in particular?" "Horse manure," came the reply. Thinking he was making progress, Rayber pressed on: "All such people have in life is the conviction they'll rise again." "They won't rise again?" Tarwater asked; "No, they won't rise again," his uncle replied, and then he brought this hopeful exchange to completion: "That's why I want you to learn all you can . . . so that you can take your place as an intelligent man in the world." But he was never convinced that the boy had shaken the influence of his great-uncle, and he knew that he himself was a key player in the struggle between enlightenment and superstition: "The boy would go either his way or old Tarwater's and he was determined to save him for the better course."

That neither young Tarwater nor Rayber himself was free of the prophetic vocation, however, becomes clear the night following this conversation. Hearing a door open and close, Rayber knew that the boy had left the house. Half-fascinated, half-terrified, he threw on a coat and followed him clandestinely, hoping to uncover some of the mystery of the boy's mind. Up and down dark streets, past huddles of threatening people, faster and faster they went, young Tarwater in the lead and Rayber behind. Finally, the boy came to a stop, directly in front of the old building they had visited earlier in the day, the one with a banner over it: "unless ye be born again. . . ." Infuriated at this regression into primitive behavior, Rayber resolved to spy out young Tarwater through a window and then roar at him to come out. In the back of the building, he found a low window and rested his chin just above the ledge and peered in. He saw a rapt crowd listening as a man and woman talked about their little daughter who had "travelled the world over telling people about Jesus," and who would soon preach to them. Immediately, Rayber's mind was conflicted. On the one hand, he bristled at the thought of "another child's mind

warped" by religion, but on the other hand, he was reminded, with
a terrible nostalgia, of his own days under the tutelage of Old Tarwater, when, born again in Christ, he had dreamed of a prophet's
vocation.

The child appeared on the stage and quickly moved into the
rhythmic eloquence of an experienced pentecostal preacher, speaking of our expectation and God's surprising response: "The world
said 'How long, O Lord, do we have to wait?' And the Lord said,
'My Word is coming, my Word is coming from the house of David,
the King.'" Then, abruptly and unexpectedly, she turned from the
glare of the lights and gazed through the window where Rayber
was gazing at her. When she saw him, "a deep shock went through
him," because "he was certain that the child had looked directly
into his heart." As she preached, turning, alternately, from the
people to the face in the window, Rayber wanted to heal her mind,
to bring her into the light, to offer her the very things he was offering to young Tarwater. At the same time, he was transfixed by her,
as though "their spirits had broken the bonds of age and ignorance
and were mingling in some unheard of knowledge of each other."
The intensity of her preaching was appealing with enormous power
to the acorn of the prophet within him, the denied and covered-
over vocation to speak the truth of God that Old Tarwater had
discerned so many years before. Like the biblical Jonah and like
young Tarwater, Rayber was caught in the maelstrom of a resisted
mission.

Then, to his horror, the child evangelist raised her arm, pointed
directly at Rayber and shrieked, "I see a damned soul before my
eye! I see a dead man Jesus hasn't raised. His head is in the window
but his ear is deaf to the Holy Word!"[19] Horrified, he slipped to the
ground and began to slap furiously at his coat and his head, trying
to turn off the hearing aid so as to drown out the accusing voice.
Finally succeeding in finding the button, he rested in the sheltering
silence and returned to the deafness that the Word of God had,
momentarily, broken through. At that moment, he spied young
Tarwater bursting out of the door of the tabernacle. Confronting
him he said sarcastically, "I hope you enjoyed the show." Embar-

rassed, the boy responded, "I only gone to spit on it." His rationalist side skeptical, his prophetic side intrigued, Rayber responded, "I'm not so sure of that."

The next day, Rayber, Bishop, and young Tarwater set out to tour a museum. On the way, they stopped in a midcity park, and the two failed prophets fell into conversation, the older trying unsuccessfully to convince the younger that the adventure of the night before was of no significance. While they talked, young Tarwater was overwhelmed with a mystical sense, as though his great-uncle were there, pressing his demand to baptize the child. And then, to the consternation of Rayber and the horror of young Tarwater, the idiot-child wandered off, delighted, in the direction of a splashing fountain situated in the middle of the park. As he frolicked in the stream of water, he was covered in the sunlight which "rested like a hand" upon "his white head." Could this be a sign? It felt as though his old great-uncle was hiding nearby, holding his breath, waiting for the prophetic act. Still torn, still undecided, young Tarwater moved tentatively toward the fountain, but just as he was about to step in, Rayber "bounded forward and snatched the dimwit out." Once more, the terrible attraction of the prophetic vocation, and the even more terrible refusal of it did battle, both subjectively and objectively.

The following day, the threesome set off for a trip into the country. Rayber had told his nephew that he simply wanted to get him out of the city, but in fact he intended to bring him to Powderhead, Old Tarwater's place, in order to confront his memories and burn out the old prophet's influence. On the way, they stopped at the Cherokee Lodge, a hostel situated by a little lake. As young Tarwater got out of the car, the first thing he noticed was the lake that "looked so unused that it might only the moment before have been set down by four strapping angels for him to baptize the child in."[20] Nature, the old man, God himself all seemed to be mocking him, tantalizing him. Later, out on the lake on a fishing expedition, Rayber told young Tarwater something terrible. Speaking of his retarded son, for whom he had no hope, he said, grinning horribly: "Once I tried to drown him." Coldly, the boy responded, "It was a failure of nerve; you didn't have the guts," but the revelation planted an idea in his mind. After this awkward exchange, their conversation took a psychoanalytic turn. Sensing the boy's deep conflict and frustration, his uncle said, "It's just as much relief to get something off your mind as off your stomach. When you tell somebody else your troubles, then they don't bother you so much. . . . God boy, you need help. You need to be saved right here now from the old man and everything he stands for. And I'm the one who can save you."[21] The man with the artificial hearing, the one who wanted to lead religious people from darkness to light, once more spoke unabashedly in the tones of modernity, offering salvation through psychological clarification. He was convinced that the boy would live a full life only when he saw through his great-uncle's influence and refused his divine calling. And like Descartes, Kant, Freud, and Jung, he proposes himself as the savior, the facilitator of this refusal.

A little later, the avatar of modernity continues in the same vein. He tells the boy bluntly that he knows the source of his confusion: "The old man told you to baptize Bishop. You have that order lodged in your head like a boulder blocking your path. . . . Until you get rid of this compulsion to baptize Bishop, you'll never make any progress toward being a normal person." He has seen into the mind of young Tarwater precisely because he himself has a similar compulsion, also inherited from the old prophet. He realizes full well that the prophetic seed has fallen into the soil of his mind: "I know it's in me," he says furiously, "but I keep it under control. I weed it out." His books, his learning, his psychological insight, his deep desire to be contemporary have all kept the acorn, the *imago Christi*, suppressed, and he wanted nothing more than to teach young Tarwater these same stratagems of denial. But the boy knew better. Mocking his uncle's attempts to stamp out the prophetic seed, he sneered, "It's you the seed fell in. It ain't a thing you can do about it. It fell on bad ground but it fell in deep." Undeterred by this outburst of robustly biblical terminology, Rayber returned to the typically modern language of knowledge and freedom: "I want you to see the choice. I want you to make the choice and not simply be driven by a compulsion you don't understand. What we understand, we can control."²² Like Adam and Eve grasping, in false freedom, at the knowledge of good and evil, Rayber, the modern man, convinces himself that salvation will come when he gets control of his life through his intellect and will. What young Tarwater, despite his hesitations, clearly sees is that this is a lie. Though he has not yet found a way to walk it, he knows, due to his great-uncle's tutelage, the third path of holiness and its implications.

The narrative now moves quickly to its climax. After the unproductive exchange between uncle and nephew, young Tarwater rose and stood at the screen door of the hostel and gazed out toward the lake. He was quickly joined by the white-haired retarded child whom he had been commanded to baptize. When young Tarwater placed his hand on the back of the boy's neck, in a gesture both tender and threatening, Rayber said, "I haven't given you permission to take Bishop out in the boat," but then he reconsidered: "but you may take him if you'll be careful." Ominously, Tarwater says, "I'll tend to him." The teenager and the child then went out onto the lake. After some time, Rayber rose and went to the window. It was so dark that he could not make out the boat or the two figures, and all he could hear was the thrum of the insects. Then, "the quiet was broken by an unmistakable bellow." The sound rose and fell and then "blared out one last time, rising out of its own momentum as if it were escaping finally, after centuries of waiting, into silence."²³ Prompted by the stranger's voice that had urged him not to bury his great-uncle, young Tarwater had drowned the idiot-child. But as he held him under the water to kill him, the prophet "cried out the words of baptism, shuddered and opened his eyes." At the last moment, just as he was snuffing out the child and thus giving the lie to his great-uncle's prediction and renouncing his vocation, he performed the act, claiming Bishop for the Father, the Son, and the Holy Ghost.

Dazed and afraid, young Tarwater then set out in the general direction of Powderhead. A tired trucker picked him up, hoping that conversation would keep him awake. The boy told him that he was hungry, and the driver pulled out a half-eaten sandwich and handed it to him. But when young Tarwater held the sandwich in his hands, he couldn't bring himself to eat it. Though he was starving, he knew that neither this sandwich nor any ordinary food would satisfy him. And then he remembered his great-uncle's insistence that the prophet feeds on the Bread of Life. When the driver pulled over and fell asleep, the hungry baptizer made his escape and continued on foot to Powderhead.

The broad road narrowed into a rutted gully, which disappeared into a blackberry thicket. He was getting closer. He came to a gap in the wood and he could spy the clearing where stood the burned out cabin and the rows of corn his great-uncle had planted. Young Tarwater seized a tree branch and, with some matches that the driver had given him, he lit it, turning it into a brand. As he moved down the decline toward the clearing, he poked the fire from time to time into the underbrush, setting the woods around him ablaze. And he began to feel anew the terrible constriction of his stomach, that familiar and insatiable hunger. Getting closer, he noticed, to his surprise, that the corn had grown a foot and that the ground around it had been recently plowed and, to his shock, that the grave that he had begun to scratch out of the ground was completed, freshly mounded and, at its head, set with a dark rough cross. Then he saw, astride a mule, the Negro Buford, who had faithfully done what the young prophet could not bring himself to do. "It's owing to me he's resting there," the black man said. "I buried him while you were laid out drunk. It's owing to me his corn has been plowed. It's owing to me the sign of his Saviour is over his head."[24]

The baptism completed, the grave dug, filled, and properly adorned, the young prophet was now ready for vision. As he stared at the empty field, "it seemed to him no longer empty but peopled with a multitude. Everywhere, he saw dim figures seated on the slope and as he gazed he saw that from a single basket the throng was being fed." Scanning the scene with care, young Tarwater finally made out the figure he was looking for: "The old man was lowering himself to the ground. When he was down and his bulk had settled, he leaned forward, his face turned toward the basket, impatiently following its progress toward him." The old prophet had taken his place among the saved and was preparing to feast on the Bread of Life, the body of Jesus, the food for everlasting life. And suddenly, the boy realized that the object of his insatiable hunger was the same as Old Tarwater's, that he too longed for the Bread of Life: "His hunger was so great that he could have eaten all the loaves and fishes after they were multiplied."[25]

And as the vision faded, he felt the hunger in him, no longer as a pain, but as a tide, "rising through the centuries . . . through time and darkness . . . building from the blood of Abel to his own, rising and engulfing him." The divine summons, heard and felt through the millennia of salvation history, by Isaiah, Jeremiah, Abraham, Moses, Elijah, Peter and Paul, was echoing in him. Throwing himself to the ground, his face against the dirt of his great-uncle's grave, he heard the command: "GO WARN THE CHILDREN OF GOD OF THE TERRIBLE SPEED OF MERCY." In that moment, fully surrendering to God, allowing the divine purpose to tie him up and take him where he would not go, young Tarwater found himself, found his life, found his mission. "The boy stooped and picked up a handful of dirt off his great-uncle's grave and smeared it on his forehead." Then, setting his face like flint, "his singed eyes" already envisioning the fate that awaited him, he moved "toward the dark city, where the children of God lay sleeping."[26] The battle was over; the struggle between uncle and great-uncle resolved; the voice of the stranger was stilled. Young Tarwater, at long last, realized that his life was not about him.

Like all Flannery O'Connor tales, this one leaves us shaken, worn out, more than a little confused. She once said, in answer to a question about the brutality of her stories, that a secular society, become insensitive to the nature of religion, had to be shocked out of its complacency by the exaggerated and the macabre. And so in this novel, she establishes the extremes of prophecy (Old Tarwater) and modernity (Rayber) and places the would-be prophet rather dramatically in the middle. Some of the first reviewers of *The Violent Bear It Away* comically misread it as a lampoon on the backwoods primitiveness of Old Tarwater and an advocacy of Rayber's common sense! In one of her letters, O'Connor herself set that reading aside: "The modern reader will identify himself with the school teacher, but it is the old man who speaks for me."[27] Stanley Hauerwas has commented that the great lie of secular modernity is that we have no story except the one that we invent for ourselves out of our freedom.[28] Rayber bought this ideology, but Old Tarwater never accepted such a nihilist reading. He knew that his life was, whether he approved or not, *storied* from the beginning, and he trained his grand-nephew by situating him within the great narrative. What becomes clear as O'Connor's drama unfolds is that the existential choice is not between having a story or not, but rather between acquiescing to one's role in it or resisting it. That is the option the stranger so starkly and correctly lays out: "It's Jesus or you."

Nowhere in the novel is it suggested that this latter choice is a simple one. That Rayber struggles is obvious, but the name "Tarwater," shared by both the old man and the boy, points to the warfare between irreconcilable tendencies within even the prophets themselves. There is the water of baptism and eternal life that is utterly unmixable with the tar of sin and resistance to grace, and both coinhere in the servant of God. And the name of Tarwater's home, "Powderhead," has a similarly ambiguous overtone. On the one hand, it signals the power (*dynamis*) which St. Paul associated with the proclamation of the Gospel, and on the other hand, it points to the volatile, explosive combustibility of the divided soul. When young Tarwater sets fire to his great-uncle's cabin at the beginning of the story and when he ignites the woods at the end, he is playing a dangerous game. Is it the Lord's will ("I have come to light a fire on the earth") or is it simply wanton, willful destruction? As always, the key is the ego's freedom. If it is clung to and exaggerated, turning inward upon itself, it becomes a poison; if it is surrendered to the higher will, turned outward to the mystery of God, it becomes luminous.

Couldn't one object that the prophetic vocation, described both in the biblical narratives and in Flannery O'Connor's story, is real

but rare, that is to say, something offered to a comparative handful of outstanding figures in salvation history? And couldn't one
contend as well, against a central argument of this book, that the
realization of the divine mission is hardly a path of holiness for the
average person, but one walked by a special few? In another of her
letters, O'Connor responds to just this sort of criticism. There are
indeed only a few prophets — Abraham, Moses, Elijah, John the
Baptist — who were entrusted with a great and dramatic mission,
but everyone has a vocation to do the will of God, even if the
contours of that mission are quite restricted. What, for example,
will young Tarwater do when he arrives in the city? O'Connor says
that he might baptize one other idiot child before he is ground up
by the opposition of the people — but that would be enough, if
such were the will of God.[29] Very much in the spirit of Balthasar,
Flannery O'Connor feels that the quality of one's mission cannot
be measured in ego-dramatic, but only in theo-dramatic, terms.

What do we make, finally, of the strange title, *The Violent Bear
It Away?* O'Connor took the phrase from the Douay-Rheims translation of Matthew 11:12: "From the days of John the Baptist until
now, the kingdom of heaven suffereth violence, and the violent
bear it away." It is a famously ambiguous passage and has given
rise to a variety of interpretations over the centuries. Many have
taken it to mean that the kingdom of God is attacked by violent people (such as those who killed John the Baptist) and that
they threaten to take it away. But others have interpreted it in
the opposite direction, as a word of praise to the spiritually violent
who manage to get into the kingdom. Flannery O'Connor herself sides with this latter group. In a letter of July 1959, she says,
"St. Thomas's gloss on this verse is that the violent Christ is here
talking about representing those ascetics who strain against mere
nature. St. Augustine concurs."[30] We must keep in mind that the
"mere nature" that classical Christianity describes is a fallen nature, one that tends away from God and his demands. Thus, the
"violent," on this reading, are those spiritually heroic types who
resist the promptings and tendencies of this nature and seek to
discipline it in various ways, in order to enter into the kingdom or

order of God. And is this not precisely the key to the story that
O'Connor tells? Rayber, the staid and rational modern, is a man
who rests complacently in his fallen nature, while Old Tarwater is
a fanatic who, with a spiritual ferociousness, and sometimes with
literal violence, opposes the ways of "mere nature." Like so many
other of O'Connor's backwoods spiritual heroes, Old Tarwater has
much in common with the ascetics of the ancient church, those
quasi-madmen who shut themselves up in desert caves or climbed
on top of pillars or starved themselves nearly to death in order to
signal to a complacent society the radicality of the Christian life.
It is not egocentric moderns who bear the kingdom, but rather the
"violent," those who realize that their lives are not about them.

The Cosmos

To this point, we have been analyzing the third path from the relatively restricted standpoint of human mission. What I would like to
do in this next section is to open things up and explore path three
from a much wider vantage point. In accordance with the dictates
of modernity, most twentieth-century Christian theology made, as
we have seen, a subjective, anthropological turn, attempting to approach the mysteries through human experience. Thus we recall
Tillich's existentialist starting point and Rahner's focus on "man
in the presence of absolute mystery." But this style — which had,
to be sure, certain advantages — largely failed to situate the drama
of individual salvation in the context of God's intense involve-
ment in the cosmos. And to miss this is to ignore huge sections
of both Bible and tradition, falling thereby into the spiritual trap
of thinking our salvation is about us. It is, therefore, seriously to
compromise the walking of path three.

From the first pages of the Bible, the sacred authors relate the
human and the cosmic, insisting that both original justice and
original sin are interwoven with the structure of the universe. For
instance, what is beautiful about Adam and Eve is made intelligible
in light of what is beautiful about all the work that God has done,
and what goes wrong with them is a consequence of a more basic

dysfunction that had crept into creation (represented by the serpent in the midst of the garden) and, in turn, has consequences for the realm of nature. Throughout the Old Testament, God's saving actions are often accompanied by signs in the heavens and on earth or involve the suspension of natural statistical probabilities. And when, in the New Testament, the savior bursts onto the scene, he addresses, not only particularly human problems such as violence, institutional oppression, and social marginalization, but also natural and cosmic ruptures such as blindness, deafness, and, ultimately, death itself. The first great Christian theologian, St. Paul, is not the least bit hesitant in drawing out the implications of Christ's salvation for a cosmos, which "groans in labor pains" (Rom. 8:22) for its day of redemption. He also sees the eschatological Christ as the head, in some sense, of all of creation, both natural and supernatural. Perhaps the most dramatic reference to the cosmic takes place in the prologue to John's Gospel, where the power at work in Jesus of Nazareth is explicitly identified with the divine logos that continually creates and sustains the whole of the universe (John 1:1–3). It was precisely these texts from Paul and John that inspired the rather remarkably nonmodern work of Pierre Teilhard de Chardin, one of the few contemporary theologians to resist the bias toward the subjective.

We find a confirmation of this biblical intuition when we look (to choose just one instance among many) at the Gothic architecture of the Middle Ages. It seems to be a primary concern of the ecclesial architects of our day to make us feel at home in churches, which often resemble cozy living rooms. But when we enter a Gothic cathedral — say, Notre Dame de Paris, Amiens, Cologne, or especially Chartres — we feel anything but cozy, for the building lifts us out of our ordinary experience and draws us into a series of new worlds. The cosmos is everywhere in the Gothic buildings, carved in the stone and fixed in the glass of the windows: trees, birds, roots and tendrils, exotic animals, insects, the planets and stars. The designers of these structures shared with their biblical forebears the conviction that all of these natural powers were stamped by the creative Logos and hence related to the Logos made flesh in Jesus.[31] Nowhere is this link to nature made more humorously clear than at Laon Cathedral. At the very top of the spires that rise from the four corners of the central tower of that church there are situated — not angels, not heroes, not biblical figures — but cows. The architects wanted to honor these animals that carried wine, food, and supplies to the work site, but they also wanted to give glory to the Logos that has assigned the humble cow an essential, if unglamorous, role in the cosmic theo-drama.

In his *Introduction to Christianity*, written just after the Second Vatican Council, Joseph Ratzinger develops an argument for God's existence that is drawn from both classical and contemporary sources and that effectively presents the divine in a cosmic perspective. Ratzinger begins with the simple observation that all things are intelligible, that is to say, marked by form.[32] Pythagoras had the same insight and said that all objects are numbered; the medieval scholastics expressed this intuition in a characteristically pithy formula: *omne ens est scibile*, all being is knowable. Einstein and other scientists on the contemporary scene have noted the mystical fact that the sciences themselves can neither verify nor explore, precisely because it is the foundation upon which they operate: the intelligibility of nature. What these authors witness to, in short, is that all existents, from quarks to black holes to archangels, have in common at least the odd fact that they *can be known*.

But, continues Ratzinger, this "objective mind," universal in scope, can be adequately explained only through recourse to a "subjective mind," that is to say, a universal Knower who stands behind it. God, in short, is that Mind that has cognized the world as we know it into existence, stamping it with form. It is interesting, Ratzinger notes, that the word we customarily use to designate the act of understanding is "recognize," literally "re-cognizing" something, thinking again what has already been thought into it. Einstein saw this and noted: "In the laws of nature, an intelligence so superior is revealed that in comparison all the significance of human thinking and human arrangements is a completely worthless reflection."[33] What this argument presents is not so much an "orderer" of the things in the cosmos as an intelligent ground of the cosmos itself. The relationship between objective intelligibility and subjective Intelligence is summed up in the first article of the Creed: "I believe in God." It is to assert "the primacy of Logos over and against mere matter."[34] Those who put their faith in God know that matter cannot be the final ground to which reality is reduced (as all forms of materialism maintain), that indeed matter itself, as informed, rests upon a mind that is more basic.

I spent time rehearsing this argument because it expresses in tight philosophical language the intuition about God and the cosmos that the Christian tradition has, from the beginning, reverenced. God is not one being among many — even the supreme being — but rather God is the Mind that undergirds and hence unites all expressions of finitude. Because all creation is marked by the divine knower, everything in creation is related in a reasonable way to God and to everything else. Just as any one point on a Cartesian coordinate system can be connected to every other point in a rationally describable way, so every creature can be connected reasonably to every other creature, though the texture of that reasonability can be fully known only to God. And just as every geometrical shape can be considered in a broader context as part of a larger and more complex configuration, so every finite thing, intelligible in itself, can and must be seen as part of greater and more far reaching patterns of intelligibility, again fully knowable only to God. St. Francis of Assisi witnessed to this cosmic connectedness when he spoke, in language both poetic and metaphysically precise, of "brother sun and sister moon."

There is no figure among the classical theologians who stresses the cosmic connection more powerfully than Thomas Aquinas. We who have become accustomed to highly psychologized and subjective accounts of theology are, undoubtedly, surprised at the innumerable references in Thomas's work to the universal setting that dwarfs and properly contextualizes the human. There is in Thomas an anticipation of what we saw in Ratzinger: a keen sense of the perfection and intelligibility of the universe that has come forth through God's creativity. But there is more. For Aquinas, "perfection" has that relatively static meaning, but it has a dynamic connotation as well, suggested in the Latin *per-factum* (having been brought to completion). In this second sense, the perfection of the universe is not a given, but rather what happens as all of the elements of creation are lured toward and attain their proper end through action. Despite the protestations of the Darwinians in the nineteenth century and so many opponents of "classical theism" today, Aquinas's universe is anything but a prim and fixed place. On the contrary, everything in it, from lowest to highest, unconsciously or consciously, is moving under the direction, and according to the purposes, of a universal divine providence.[35]

Thomas uses a variety of metaphors to express this corporate mobility. The world, he tells us, is like a household, made up of numerous persons of differing rank, each contributing to the overall functioning of the place, at the command of a *paterfamilias* who sets the tone and establishes the end. Or it is like an army, composed of thousands of soldiers, officers, and support personnel, all under the direction of a commanding general moving them to a shared goal.[36] The dominant themes are purposiveness, interdependence, rational structure, and, above all, mobility: a household is a bustling place, and an army is on the move. What is perhaps especially helpful about these metaphors is how they illumine the various levels of order and understanding that exist in complex corporate structures. A farmhand can be usefully at work at the behest of his immediate superior and understand perfectly what he is doing, though he might be completely unaware of how the performance of his task contributes to an overall design envisioned by the *paterfamilias*. Or a platoon commander in Eisenhower's army can dutifully carry out an order from the general to establish a particular beachhead, without for a moment grasping the broadest context for that action. So in the household of the universe, the mission of an obscure human being, following her perception of God's will, can interact in stunningly complex ways with the "missions" of trees, plants, angels, and other human beings in response to the promptings of the divine *Paterfamilias*. And in the army of the cosmos, one person's brave acceptance of a mission that ends in his own death can open up a series of events that contribute to the overall battle plan of the divine commander.

Another Thomistic metaphor for God's cosmic providence — invoked time and again in his writings — is that of the artist and the work of art.[37] Like a painter or sculptor, God raises in his mind the image of what he wants to make and then, through a disciplined act of creativity, brings that idea to material expression. But though we can appreciate particular masterpieces that God has wrought, we must remember that the ultimate canvas that God is painting, the final block of marble that God is carving, is the whole of creation, across space and time. Thus, as we survey the world from our necessarily limited perspective, we are like visitors walking through a sculptor's studio. We see some finished pieces, but we also see, amid the inevitable clutter of a workplace, many sculptures half-finished, or barely started, or only vaguely outlined. And as we puzzle over this figure and that, we certainly have no sense of the massive work of which all of these will one day be a part, in accordance with the artist's design. Or we are like a person surveying Georges Seurat's pointillist masterpiece *Sunday Afternoon on la Grande Jatte* with his nose pressed against the canvas. That picture reveals its meaning only as one steps back from it, and the colors begin to blend and the lights and darks gradually arrange themselves into patterns. What we see of God the Artist's work are bits and pieces in his studio or one tiny corner of his endlessly complex pointillist canvas. Dante expresses this same idea at the very end of the *Divine Comedy*. As he stares into the beauty of the Trinity at the end of his pilgrimage, Dante sees

> how it contains within its depths
> all things bound in a single book by love
> of which creation is the scattered leaves.[38]

This event, that relationship, this heartbreak, that victory — these are the pages from various sections of one great book. Only when the whole plot is unfolded do we see how each finds its place in the story.

We might follow this Dantean suggestion and develop a final

metaphor of Author and novel. Fiction writers tell us that, though they design and, to some degree, determine the moves of their characters, they also watch those characters and record, with delight and surprise, what they do. They also fall in love with their creations: Dickens admitted that he wept when describing the deaths of certain of his favorite characters. God the creator is like the author of a book involving setting, plot, and players endowed with freedom. In one sense, God is responsible for everything in his book; it all comes forth as he intended, from his mind. But in another sense, God watches as his characters act out their roles, in perhaps surprising and frustrating ways. And like an author passionately involved in his story, God cheers on, cajoles, weeps with, and delights in his characters. Given God's power and fidelity, we know the ultimate end of his story — it is a divine comedy — but the exact playing out of the drama involving all of humanity, all of nature, and all of the cosmos remains flexible and unpredictable.

All of these cosmic metaphors shed some light on the theological problem of problems, namely, the puzzle of evil. Why does the thoroughly good God permit so much shadow in his creation? Perhaps the difficulty is not so much the elusiveness of the answer as the question itself, based as it is on the assumption that we can grasp what "evil" and "good" really mean. From our infinitely restricted point of vantage, we are in no position to assess, with any degree of accuracy, just how the pages of the great book fit together, or just how the strategic moves of the army conduce to victory, or just how the colors, both bright and somber, contribute to the design. And therefore, it is presumptuous of us to pose the dilemma: How can God's goodness be reconciled with obvious evil? Could it be that God's goodness is more terrible than we can grasp, and the consequences of "evil" more wonderful than we can see? Isn't it significant that the original sin of our first parents is described in Genesis as the reaching for just this sort of definitive grasp of the nature of good and evil? And isn't it worth noting that, in the book of Job, the Old Testament's most powerful presentation of this problem, we find, not so much an answer, but a disciplining of the question in light of a cosmic consciousness (Job 42:1–6)?

I would like to close this necessarily inadequate meditation on the deepest theological problem there is by talking about two dogs. Imagine, first, with C. S. Lewis, a dog wandering through a street on the outskirts of Hiroshima during the late morning of August 6, 1945. He sees a flash of light and is then knocked to the ground by a blast of heat. Struggling to his feet a few minutes later, he moves on, limping now and unable to see out of one eye. He suffers and, within the framework of his canine consciousness, he "grasps" his suffering. But never, even in principle, could he begin to understand that his suffering was the result of a terrible war among beings at a higher plane of existence. This higher plane had impinged upon his world, but he remains, necessarily, oblivious to its texture. Or follow William James's suggestion and imagine a dog wandering into your library at home. He sees everything there — the globe, the newspapers, the array of brightly colored and elaborately decorated books — but he grasps none of it, has no inkling of the worlds present in that room. So, says James, are we in the cosmos that we inhabit. We see it all — its joys and sorrows, its colors bright and somber — but we have little or no insight into the higher world that contextualizes it and appears within it.

One of the most popular spiritual books of recent years has been *The Celestine Prophecy*. It recounts a story that is, at once, an adventure tale and a journey of the soul — and it involves the weaving-together of a wide variety of religious and philosophical themes. But the motif that dominates the book is a cosmic one, that of the meaningful coincidence. That a person happens to encounter this woman at this time, under these circumstances, against this background, is seen, not as a mere happenstance, but as an opportunity for greater life and growth. Or when a particular question is burning in the mind of one character, he finds himself, seemingly by chance, back-to-back in a waiting room with a perfect stranger, and it becomes clear that he is "meant" to talk to this man, who has the answer he is looking for. In the end, *The Celestine Prophecy* argues that there are no pure coincidences, that all has its place in the unfolding cosmic story. Now I realize that all of this can sound a bit strained and new-agey, but I would call to mind Greeley's law. What I found as I read this book was a "picking up" of a very old theme in classical Christian spirituality, namely, the universal influence of divine providence. Aquinas teaches that God, the sustaining cause of creation, actively guides all things to their proper end; God is, as we have seen, general, *paterfamilias*, author, artist. But these images imply that nothing escapes providence, that everything is part of the complex working out of God's plan. Therefore, though from the limited standpoint of the nexus of contingent causes, we can speak of chance and luck and accident, from the standpoint of the cause of causes, such language is inappropriate. Everything that happens is, either by direction or permission, an expression of the divine will, and thus everything should be seen by the attentive disciple as an opportunity and an offer.

Jean-Pierre de Caussade, eighteenth-century Jesuit spiritual director, based his spirituality on this simple principle. In his writings and talks, he developed the one great idea that everything that happens to us in the course of a day — from the people we meet, to the weather, to the appearance of a beautiful vista, to an insulting word — is revelatory of the will of God.[39] When this insight is accepted by the mind and sensed by the heart, one's life radically changes, for the whole of it now becomes charged with meaning and the possibility of adventure. Our divine mission — like Tarwater's — is held out in all people, good or evil, in all events, pleasant or unpleasant, in all meetings, fortunate or otherwise. Over all of those too easy dichotomies we must place the qualification of the divine will; both customary "good" and "evil" are transformed when they are placed in the higher context of God's overarching providence. A few years ago, when I was beginning an eight-day Jesuit retreat, my director said, "Spend the first day reflecting on all of the positive things that have happened to you in the course of your life — and thank God for all of it." When I returned the next morning and reported to him the fruits of that meditation, he said, "Good, now spend the second day reflecting on all of the agonies and trials of your life — and thank God for those too."

And this idea is presented from beginning to end of the Bible. For the sacred authors of the Old Testament, God is implicated in everything that happens (and doesn't happen) to the Israelites. They never argue that God is active in Israel's good fortune and inactive when Israel suffers, provident in the first case and indifferent or powerless in the second. On the contrary, whether the chosen people triumph or fall, in their battles both victorious and disastrous, during David's majestic empire and during the Babylonian captivity, in Job's comfort and Job's anguish, *God acts*. To be sure, God's action is varied, strange, unpredictable, but the one thing it is not is occasional. And this intuition unambiguously informs the authors of the New Testament texts as well. The will of God is displayed in the whole course of Jesus' life, both in the "Galilean springtime" of his success and especially in the "folly" and "stumbling block" of his cross. In sum, the biblical question is never "Is God speaking?" but rather "What is God saying?"

Practices for Path Three

Discerning the Will of God

Earlier in the book, I insisted that, for Christians, God is not simply "out there" like a mountain waiting to be climbed by the intrepid spiritual mountaineer; rather, God is himself a pursuer, hunting us down with relentless love. I might shift the image a bit and suggest that God is not only behind us in pursuit, but also ahead of us in allurement, like a mother urging her child to take his first steps. Alfred North Whitehead argued that God is the great displayer of possibilities for his universe, the one who arranges and rearranges persons, objects, and events in the hopes that his creation might come to richer and more creative expression. During the discourse he gave the night before he died, Jesus summed up his life and ministry in these words: "I have said these things that my joy may be in you and your joy may be complete" (John 15:11). And therefore Christians walking the third path confidently and enthusiastically *look*. They know that God is luring them and so they hunt for signs. This process of watching and listening is an ancient ecclesial practice called "discernment."

One of the best guides in this practice is the twentieth-century Jesuit scholar Bernard Lonergan, for, as an academician, he specialized in questions of method (hunting down the truth) and, as a Jesuit, he was trained in the discernment of spirits (hunting down the will and movement of God). At the heart of Lonergan's method is a process that he expressed in terms of four imperatives: (1) be attentive; (2) be intelligent; (3) be reasonable; and (4) be responsible.[40] Let us examine these by turn. By "attention," Lonergan means something very simple and, in practice, very elusive: seeing what is there to be seen. Seeing, not selectively, myopically, or superficially, but really taking in the light, colors, shapes, and objects that surround one. For Lonergan, many scientists go off the rails, not because they lack speculative intelligence, but because they get their data wrong, they don't *look*. What does this mean for Christians on path three? It means that they take seriously what Aquinas said concerning God's immanence in all things, "by essence, presence, and power," and that they see, consequently, everything as saturated with the divine. Many of the spiritual masters have defined prayer, not as an escape from the ordinary, but as a kind of heightened attention to the depth dimension of the everyday and the commonplace. Where is the divine will displayed? For the one who has the discipline of vision, everywhere and in everything. For many, the spiritual life becomes dysfunctional precisely at this beginning stage — they don't look.

The next step in Lonergan's method is the act of intelligence. By this he means the seeing of patterns, or what, in more classical philosophy, are called forms. Some people are extremely attentive, taking in thoroughly even the details of what goes on around them, but they are not intelligent, that is to say, they are not curious about the patterns of meaning that give coherence and order to what they have perceived. The grasping of intelligible structure is what Lonergan calls "insight."[41] It corresponds to the "ah-ha" moment, the sudden turning-on of the light, the "eureka!"-inducing grasp of meaning. In a scientific context, intelligence undergirds the form-

Realizing Your Life Is Not about You

ing of hypotheses or plausible explanations for phenomena; in a more interpersonal or psychological framework, it motivates the proposal of theories to explain behavior patterns; in a philosophical setting, it compels the relentless asking of the question, "why?"

How does this second move of the mind play itself out in a properly spiritual context? Having taken in the world around them, confident that God is present in all things, intelligent Christians now seek to discern the patterns, to know precisely what God is up to. In this process, they utilize the lenses of the biblical and theological tradition, having insight by aligning their experience to the Great Story of divine revelation. Guided by the patterns of creation — exodus, prophecy, vocation, sin and grace, Incarnation, death and resurrection, second-coming — they seek analogies and correspondences to their own story. Thus, as Moses was to Pharaoh, so I am to an oppressive employer; as Yahweh treated the Israelites during their exile, so God is treating me during my depression; as Jesus commissioned his disciples to preach, so I feel a commission to proclaim the word to my family. Picasso once said that the key to his artistic genius was the capacity to see visual analogies: the shape of that pear is like the contour of a guitar, which is like the curve of a woman's body, etc. The intelligent Christian discerner must have the like capacity to see these analogies (similarities in difference) between the biblical and the experienced. Now just as the scientist or philosopher is trained through a long process of apprenticeship to see certain patterns, so the religious seeker must be trained through a long immersion in the universe of the Bible. This has happened over the centuries, as I have been arguing throughout this book, in icons, the lives of the saints, cathedrals, poems, songs, and especially the liturgy. The Christian community learns the practice of intelligent discernment through all of these means.

The third step in Lonergan's process is the hard-edged and decisive move of reasonability or judgment. Having surveyed perhaps an entire series of bright ideas, the reasonable person must now decide which is the right idea. All hypotheses, almost by definition, are interesting, but only one of them is adequate to the case and the evidence. At the second level of intelligence, playfulness is altogether in order, for sometimes the most outrageous hypothesis is the correct one. When looking for insights, one should be expansive, wide-ranging, imaginative, even a little silly. But when seeking to make a judgment, one has to be clear, hard, and censorious: there is, after all, only one truly right answer. Many people, Lonergan thinks, are wonderfully attentive and insightful, but, they lack this crucial third intellectual quality of discrimination: they can never finally make up their minds.

Discerning Christians have to move through this third phase as well. They see God's work and will in all that surrounds them; they apply a whole series of biblical grids, seeking to relate their story to the Great Story; now, they must decide precisely what God is saying and how God is luring them. Monitoring and encouraging this third step is essential in the work that I do in a seminary context. The men that I deal with are those who are trying, in a very conscious way, to discover how God is calling them. Is it priesthood or not? It can't be both, and they know it. A judgment, in either direction painful, has to be made, and they know that too. Often, as they entertain patterns for their lives in relation to God, a number of attractive possibilities emerge, and this multiplicity of scenarios makes the judgment that much more wrenching. But what seminarians do in a particularly focused way is what all responsible Christians must do. The Flannery O'Connor novel that we examined earlier is nothing but a dramatic presentation of this third step of discernment. Having been introduced to two grids for understanding his life — his great-uncle's biblical vision and his uncle's rationalist one — young Tarwater had to judge which was right. As the stranger reminded him: "It's either Jesus or you."

And this is the rub. How do we make this all-important judgment, one that touches not simply on what we are to do but who we are to be? How do we know? Scientists proceed in their task by way of controlled experimentation, carefully eliminating hypotheses until they arrive at the most persuasive; and there is something similar in the arena of the spiritual. The discerning and reasonable disciple of Jesus can also employ a process of elimination, setting aside, gradually, various inadequate patterns. Thus, when determining what God wants me to do, I can certainly eliminate a pattern of life that is at odds with the central narratives and symbols of revelation, say a life governed by sensuality, self-absorption, or violence. More pointedly, I can rule out a life that is inconsistent with the basic pattern of Jesus' life; somehow I know that, whatever form my vocation takes, it will be, essentially, Christoform. Thus, for example, a pattern of existence that is predicated on the assumptions that there is no life after death or that enemies should not be loved would be necessarily inadequate. But having negated these rather obviously problematic hypotheses, how do I proceed in the face of a variety of Christologically viable options?

Here the discernment must become more refined. One of the best guides is in the fifth chapter of Paul's letter to the Galatians. Jesus had said that a tree is known by its fruits, and Paul makes this very specific. He tells us that the fruits of the Holy Spirit are "love, joy, peace, patience, kindness, generosity, faithfulness, gentleness, and self-control" (Gal. 5:22–23), implying that the Spirit's presence in one's life can be read from its radiance in these soul-expanding qualities. Earlier, I spoke of the *magna anima* (the great soul) of the saint in contrast to the *pusilla anima* (the cramped soul) of the sinner. All of Paul's "fruits of the Spirit" are marks of an expansive and outward-looking *magna anima*. Love is willing the good of another; joy is diffusive of itself; patience bears with the troublesome; kindness makes the other gentle; generosity benefits the neighbor; faithfulness is a dedication to a partner or friend; self-control restricts the havoc that the ego can cause. Which vocation ought to be mine? The one that awakens in me these attributes; the one that makes great my soul.

Now how do I know that my life is, in fact, bearing these fruits? It is most helpful to consult the Christian community. Just as in Dante our sins are more easily spied by those around us, so our virtues and charisms are often most clearly seen by our colleagues and companions. Therefore, we should listen carefully to others as we discern God's path for us. John Henry Newman insists that the *sensus fidelium* ought to be consulted even in matters of doctrine;[42]

how much more ought this feel of the community be investigated in the determination of vocation.

Another powerful aid in discernment is honest and hopeful prayer. Over and again in the Scripture we are urged to pray, asking God even for the simplest things. In the New Testament virtually the only kind of prayer taught is the prayer of petition, and we are encouraged to pray ceaselessly, relentlessly. The Lord's Prayer, for example, is nothing but a string of eight requests, and we say it over and again in the course of the Christian life. Thus, when seeking to know the path, ask. And then ask again. And ask a third time. Then have the imagination and focus to look for the answer. Since God loves to work clandestinely, through a series of secondary causes, it is altogether possible that he is providing an answer to our prayer in the ordinary events, conversations, and people around us. But we must be attentive to these signs.

Lonergan's final step is that of responsibility. Once we have been attentive, intelligent, and reasonable, we must, finally, accept the full implications of the true judgment we have made. Now we must adjust our lives in light of the truth that we have discovered, no matter how uncomfortable that adjustment may be. As Lonergan well knew, many people fall precisely at this point: they have followed the process admirably and have made a correct judgment, but they just cannot bring themselves to act on it. Politicians judge that backing a particular bill is morally wrong, but they do it because of the desire to be reelected; or researchers discover a particular truth but fail to publish their findings for fear of losing their funding. I have known seminarians who clearly knew that they were called by God to the priesthood, but who opted not to become priests. And I have known those who determined, by a careful process, that they ought not to be priests and became ordained anyway. Both sets of people tended to go into tailspins.

And so Christian disciples, on the path of discernment, must abide by Lonergan's fourth imperative. They must have the courage of their Christian convictions and place in their body the truth that they have accepted. In some ways, this entire book — with its emphasis on embodied practice — has been an exhortation to make this indispensable move. But how can this step be encouraged? Here again, I would emphasize the importance of the Christian community. As members of a living body, we bear each other's burdens, just as one bodily system will compensate for the weakness of another. Thus, one person compels — by words, gestures, cajoling, and, in extreme circumstances, sanctions — the integration of knowledge and action in another. Frequently in the Scripture, we are urged to warn a brother or sister away from a sinful path, to correct and encourage in the direction of virtue. Another way that we do this is through prayer on behalf of one another. The Irish Dominican poet Paul Murray reported this line from his own spiritual director: "Paul, I'm praying for you; so take great risks!"

The Corporal and Spiritual Works of Mercy

Dorothy Day once said that everything a baptized person does should be, directly or indirectly, related to the corporal and spiritual works of mercy: feed the hungry, give drink to the thirsty, clothe the naked, shelter the homeless, visit the imprisoned, visit the sick, bury the dead (the corporal works); counsel the doubtful, instruct the ignorant, admonish sinners, bear patiently the troublesome, comfort the afflicted, forgive offenses, pray for the living and the dead (the spiritual works). What Dorothy Day proposes here is an extremely "thick" description of the Christian life. Following Jesus is not, for her, a matter of inner states or private convictions, still less an embrace of gassy abstractions such as "peace and justice." Rather it is a set of very definite, embodied practices, things that one *does* on behalf of another. The scriptural warrant for the corporal works is, of course, the twenty-fifth chapter of Matthew's Gospel: "Lord, when was it that we saw you hungry and gave you food, or thirsty and gave you something to drink? And when was it that we saw you a stranger and welcomed you or naked and gave you clothing? ... And the king will answer them, 'Truly I tell you, just as you did it to one of the least of these who are members of my family, you did it to me'" (Matt. 25:37–40).

Feeding *this particular* hungry person and visiting *these* lonely prisoners and taking care of *this* homeless man with one's own resources — that is the form of the Christian life. Day was uneasy with the Roosevelt-era New Deal reforms, not because she lacked compassion, but because she feared that they allowed Christians to abdicate responsibility for caring directly for the needy. Applying the Catholic principle of subsidiarity, she insisted that towns, communities, families, and villages should support the brothers and sisters that they could see with their own eyes and reach with their own hands — and not pass the buck to the far more abstract care of the government. When starry-eyed young idealists would come to her Catholic Worker House, hoping to have a romantic experience "with the poor," Dorothy Day would tell them, "There are two things you need to know about the poor: they are ungrateful and they smell." The poor, she was telling them, are not a quaint abstraction, and working with them is not a holiday; their plight is frighteningly real, and the work is dangerously direct.

What we see in both the corporal and spiritual works is a practical antidote to Augustine's *curvatus in se.* All of them compel a self-regarding ego outward in the direction of mission and connection, and, as such, they constitute a distinctively Christian social theory, radically out of step with modern social arrangements, but well-suited to the walking of the third path of holiness. It is remarkably difficult to cling to the illusion that your life is about you when you are focused, body and soul, on the needs of another.

Modern social theory was born in the thought of the seventeenth-century English political philosopher Thomas Hobbes. Having bracketed the doctrine of a creator God in whom all things participate, Hobbes speculated, correctly enough, that the basic form of human life is antagonistic, the "war of all against all."[43] Disconnected to God and to each other, every human being is simply a bundle of passions to be satisfied and fears to be quelled. The supreme passion is the lust for the preservation of life, and the consummate fear is the terror of violent death. The first leads to antagonism (since we all want for ourselves the limited goods of the earth), and the second leads to the grudging compromise of social life (since it is better to surrender some individual liberty in order to protect one's life). The undergirding assumption of the entire

program is the primacy of the self-absorbed individual. Though this
Hobbesian view is softened a bit in the thought of John Locke,
the basic form remains, even in Locke, the same. It was, of course,
this Lockean form of Hobbesianism that strongly influenced the
founding fathers of the United States, especially Thomas Jefferson.
It is therefore not surprising that the dominant political idea in the
Declaration of Independence is individual rights and the protection
of those prerogatives through government. What is assumed by our
civil religion is a fundamentally antagonistic social ontology.

But this is precisely what the practice of the corporal and
spiritual works — predicated on a radically different ontology —
negates. We bear each other's burdens in love because we are,
whether we like it or not, connected to one another. Since Christians believe that we are all rooted in the same divine source, we
are all brothers and sisters, or better, organs in the same body.
Contra Hobbes, it is not the war of all against all that is "natural" to us; rather that frightening condition is the product of a
sinful denial of what the universe really is. Christians know that
when we deal with one another in love, we are not only acting in
an ethically upright manner, but we are moving in sync with the
deepest rhythms of creation. Hence, there is, for followers of Jesus,
no such thing as "your" problem; as yours it is mine. If there is one
person starving, the whole body suffers; if there is one child lonely,
we are all diminished; if there is one who dies through violence,
we are all violated. Bob Dylan commented bitterly on the typically
modern reversal of this perspective when he said, "I heard one person starve / I heard many people laughin'."[44] An uncompromised
solidarity and communion is what the works of mercy embody.

Nonviolence

Stanley Hauerwas, one of the great prophets of nonviolence in
our time, has on his office door a sign that reads: "A modest proposal for peace: Christians stop killing other Christians." In the
two world wars of the last century, killing on a scale never before
imagined in human history took place, for the most part, *among
Christians*. Between 1914 and 1945, millions of British, Canadian,

American, French, Russian, German, and Italian Christians went
at one another murderously. One presumes that the overwhelm-
ing majority of these warriors had heard Christ's command to love
even your enemies and that they had been formed according to the
doctrine of the mystical body of Christ. Yet, when the moment of
truth arrived, they chose to place national loyalty above spiritual
conviction, attacking other members of the body of Jesus for political ends. One reason why Christianity is suffering so in Europe and
why Western Christianity in general is proving so evangelically ane-
mic is, I submit, this disedifying display of violence so completely
out of step with the lifestyle recommended in the Gospels. What is
particularly compelling about Hauerwas's proposal is that it urges,
very simply, an honesty and consistency among Christians themselves. Before they even get around to loving or evangelizing their
enemies, at the very least they ought to love one another, brothers
and sisters in the same family; before they dare to teach others
the way of peace, they ought to stop tearing themselves apart. A
first (and giant) step in the direction of universal peace, in other
words, is the practice of nonviolence in the community of Christ's
disciples.

   Why do I place this practice of nonviolence on the third path
of holiness? I do so because, like the corporal and spiritual works,
nonviolence is deeply rooted in a Christian sense of creation and
connectedness. Though a complete discussion of this complex issue
would take us beyond the scope of this book, it is certainly clear
that, from very early in the theological tradition, Christian thinkers
speak of God's creation as taking place *ex nihilo* (from nothing).
And we find this teaching confirmed in all of the great theologians
from Augustine to Karl Rahner. What I would like to effect is a
correlation between this high philosophical claim and the radicality of the Paschal Mystery explored in the last chapter. We saw
that Jesus, in speaking peace to those who had betrayed and killed
him, opened up a new conception of God, one who brings order,
not through violence, but through compassion. Accordingly, when
Christians began to reflect on the nature of creation, they speculated that this true God of Jesus Christ brings the world into being,

not through an orgy of violence, as in so many of the ancient myths, but precisely through a sheerly nonviolent act of generous love. To make the universe *ex nihilo* is to bring it forth without competition, antagonism, or violence — fighting nothing, wresting nothing into shape, pressing nothing to the ground.[45] And more to the point, as Thomas Aquinas and others point out, this nonviolent act of God is not a once and for all event at the beginning of time; rather, it is the ongoing, continual act by which the world, at every moment, is sustained in existence. Hence divine nonviolence is the actualizing and unifying energy of all of creation.

And therefore when we walk in the path of nonviolence we are, as Gandhi knew, claiming and unleashing a "truth force" (*Satyagraha*), participating in an energy that runs through the cosmos in all its dimensions.[46] This is why, of course, nonviolence, when effectively practiced is remarkably powerful. In the century just concluded, the bloodiest on record, nonviolent methods liberated the subcontinent of India, effected a massive social change in the United States, and, most stunningly, brought down a Communist empire defended by an enormous military establishment. In his recent writings, Michael Baxter, a theologian strongly marked by the Catholic Worker philosophy, has revived Peter Maurin's clarion call to a church grown lukewarm: "We have taken the dynamite of the church, wrapped it in clever phraseology, placed it in hermetically sealed containers and have sat on the lids. The time has come to blow up some of the dynamite of the church." For Maurin, as for his colleague Dorothy Day, this dynamite is the practice of nonviolence. Paul said that the proclamation of the Gospel of Jesus crucified and risen from the dead is *dynamis* (power) to a cosmos in need of transformation, and this Gospel is nothing but the good news of God's nonviolent love. When we Christians announce it and, more to the point, live it, we tap into the divine *dynamis* which overmatches any of the powers of the world.

But what exactly is nonviolence? We have certainly seen faces of it in the course of our discussion. Forgiveness, truth-telling, and the works of mercy are all modes of a nonviolent lifestyle. In the Gospel sense, nonviolence is a third way between or above the

two classical responses to evil: fight and flight. In the face of oppression or attack, one can, according to common wisdom, either
fight back or run away. In the first case, as history has unambiguously and sadly shown, violence simply increases, since vengeance
begets vengeance; and in the second case, violence is allowed to
thrive since it is not opposed. Gospel love is a third path — neither
violent nor acquiescent. It actively and provocatively opposes violence, but not through more violence, fighting fire with fire, as it
were. Rather, it opposes evil through compassionate and forgiving
noncooperation; it refuses to live in the world favored by the violent person. Walter Wink's analysis of the Sermon on the Mount
is especially helpful here.[47] When Jesus told his followers to turn
the other cheek, for example, he was not recommending passivity
or acquiescence, but rather provocative noncooperation. In first-
century Palestine, a Jew would never use his left hand for any sort
of social intercourse, since it was considered unclean. Thus, if, as
Matthew's version has it, "someone slaps you on the right cheek,"
he is striking you with the back of his hand, a gesture of contempt
reserved for those deemed inferior. So when Jesus recommends, in
that case, the turning of the left cheek, he is urging his listeners
to stand nonaggressively, but defiantly, in the face of aggression,
signaling their refusal to accept the violent assumptions of their
attackers. This form of resistance, at its best, shames the aggressors
into redemptive self-knowledge, compelling them to see what their
violence has done to the other. And in this, nonviolence battles
violence but refuses to give up on the violent.

On his first trip to his native Poland as pope, John Paul II addressed a crowd of several million in the capital city of Warsaw.
As he spoke of the abiding truths of the Gospel concerning God
and the human spirit, he was interrupted by something surprising.
Inspired by the pope's message and presence, the people began to
shout, in the face of their Communist leaders, "We want God; we
want God; we want God."[48] On and on it went, like a chant or a
litany for a full thirteen minutes. Those who were there witness to
its emotional impact and saw in it the beginning of the Solidarity
movement, which galvanized the Polish resistance, which led to

the liberation of Eastern Europe, which conduced, eventually, to the breakdown of the Soviet Union. All in that brilliant moment of nonviolent resistance. The cry "we want God" seemed to call on that universal and cosmic power that undergirds the universe and overwhelms whatever stands against it.

Now just as the Master was opposed, so his nonviolent disciples will be opposed. A culture organized around the practices of aggression will actively oppose a culture predicated on the nonviolence of God, and this is why we are urged in the sixth chapter of Ephesians to arm ourselves with the whole armory of God. "Stand therefore, and fasten the belt of truth around your waist, and put on the breastplate of righteousness. As shoes for your feet put on whatever will make you ready to proclaim the Gospel of peace. With all of these, take the shield of faith.... Take the helmet of salvation, and the sword of the Spirit, which is the word of God" (Eph. 6:14–17). The Christian community is a band of nonviolent warriors, ready for battle, but armed, not with the weapons of the world, but those of Christ. The "belt of truth" with which we are girded evokes the deep truth of things: we will be successful when we align our minds and bodies to the nonviolent energy of creation. The "breastplate of righteousness" implies that we are protected by a power not our own. In the Pauline literature, "righteousness" or "justification" is always a quality that comes to us as a gift from the Lord. When we live centered in Christ's power, realizing our lives are not about us, we are protected in the war that we fight. On our feet we place the shoes of the Gospel of peace. This means that we cannot walk in the worldly ways of violence but rather in the way opened up by the nonviolence of the Paschal Mystery. The last recommendation is probably the most important. We are urged to "take the sword of the Spirit, which is the Word of God." In the book of Revelation, John sees a vision of the risen Jesus, and, proceeding from the mouth of the Lord, is a large, double-edged sword (Rev. 1:16). This is a signal that the greatest power (*dynamis*) for both attack and defense is the Word which is Jesus. Just as God creates by the power of his Word (Gen. 1:2), so he redeems by his Word. When the Christian community is seized by that divine pronouncement and allows itself to be shaped by it, it is an effective warrior-family.

During the late 1930s, as it was becoming unambiguously clear that Hitler was viciously persecuting the Jews, Jacques Maritain — Catholic philosopher, advisor to the Vatican, husband to a Jewish wife — made a striking suggestion. He said that Pope Pius XI ought to mount a donkey and ride it into Berlin, as Christ rode into Jerusalem in advance of his passion, in order to protest the Nazi policies. Would the pope have been arrested, laughed at, imprisoned, killed? Who knows. But it would have been a gesture of great *dynamis*: this single man, bereft of any of the weapons of the world, but arrayed with the full armor of God, riding off to face the enemy. The whole issue of the practice of nonviolence always brings to my mind what is perhaps Chesterton's best-known quotation: "The Christian ideal has not been tried and found wanting; it has been found difficult and left untried." So lulled are we Christians by the presuppositions and strategies of the sinful world that we never even attempt to live the radical life which Jesus has opened for us: loving our enemies into friends and our violent society into peace.

The Liturgy

The final practice I propose for path three is one that relates, in a sense, to the other two paths as well, for it is, as the Vatican Council II document *Sacrosanctum Concilium* put it, "the source and summit of the Christian life."[49] It is the action that most fully displays who we Christians — centered, sinners, and sent — distinctively are. I am speaking, of course, of the liturgy. When Thomas Merton was ordained a priest, he invited a number of his friends, many of them non-Catholic, to attend his first Mass. One of them, Seymour Freedgood, a Jew, asked the new priest, "What exactly *is* the Mass?" Expecting a more or less pietistic answer, Freedgood was surprised when Merton responded, "It is a kind of ballet, with similar prescribed movements and gestures."[50] I have always savored Merton's answer because it captures the iconic/artistic dimension of the liturgy; in its gathering, singing, signing, reading, listening, praying, offering, processing, communicating, sending and being sent, the body of Christ iconically acts out who it is — to the glory of God and for the transformation of the world.

In the book of Revelation, the visionary John is offered a glimpse of heaven. He sees a throne room, where a King sits in splendor, surrounded by a group of robed elders who perform acts of worship and obeisance. He also spies an altar, candlesticks, myriads of saints waving palm branches, the Lamb of God "standing as though slain" (Rev. 5:6), who opens a sacred text, and an angel who swings a large censer. It is hard to avoid the conclusion that we are dealing here with what the Fathers called "the heavenly liturgy," the ballet of praise that takes place in God's eternal household. What the mainstream of the Christian tradition has preserved is the conviction that when we gather for praise of God we are doing much more than merely seeking inspiration or fellowship. We are in fact consciously aligning ourselves to the celestial dance, hoping that some of its peacefulness, beauty, and order might become ours, that God's will be done "on earth as it is in heaven." We are imitating the great Practice which is eternal life.

Let us look at several dimensions of the liturgical act. The book of Revelation tells us that around God's throne are "a great multitude that no one could count, from every nation, from all tribes and peoples and languages" (Rev. 7:9). When Dorothy Day was experiencing a religious awakening and began to attend Mass on a regular basis, she was especially struck by the egalitarian and inclusive way that people gathered for the liturgy. The usual social distinctions, she noticed, were blurred, as rich and poor, educated and ignorant, members of establishment families and immigrants all came together in the same place for the same purpose. The assembled community, the body of Christ, in which there is "no longer Jew or Greek, there is no longer slave or free, there is no longer male or female" (Gal. 3:28), is itself a countercultural sign, a challenge to the antagonistic social ontology we spoke of earlier.

The prayer itself formally begins with the sign of the cross, the invocation of the Trinitarian persons. We remember that the Christian prays, not so much to God, as *inside* of God, from within the

love of Father, Son, and Holy Spirit. And so the liturgical ballet
commences with an evocation of this divine *communio* (the Father
forgetting himself in love for the Son, the Son emptying himself
in love for the Father, the Spirit the mutual breathing forth of
the love of Father and Son) and the hope that we might learn to
move in accord with its rhythms. In the symbol of Christ's cross,
we nestle within the space opened up by the Trinitarian persons
and thus find our deepest center. Next, the community consciously
engages in a path-two practice. They sing *Kyrie eleison, Christe eleison, Kyrie eleison* (Lord have mercy, Christ have mercy, Lord have
mercy), three times admitting sinfulness, three times asking for the
divine transformation. Christians in liturgical prayer are compelled
to acknowledge that their *communio* is incomplete, that it is an inadequate icon of God's *communio*. But we remember that it is only
the centered saint who can say, "Lord, have mercy."

Next, the Scriptures are read. Christians stand firmly in the
Pauline tradition that *fides ex auditu*, faith comes from hearing.
The assumptions of subjectivizing modernity notwithstanding, they
know that faith does not well up from common human experience
or from the structures of the psyche, but rather comes from without as a revelation, literally an unveiling, of a truth that would be
otherwise unavailable. Christians discover who God is, what con-
stitutes the sacred world, who they are and ought to be, precisely
by listening to the oddly textured narratives of the Bible. They
learn to be holy by attending to the cast of characters — saints,
rogues, prophets, sinners — on display in the biblical stories, and
especially by watching the great Character who acts, sometimes
directly, sometimes indirectly, in every story. The homily or sermon effects a correlation between this biblical narrative and the
experience of the community. Mind you, it is not a correlation in
a Tillichean sense, bringing together secular questions and sacred
answers; rather it is a drawing up of the lived world into the biblical patterns, or a laying of the latter on the former as a kind of
interpretive grid. As they listen to the Word in the liturgical assembly, Christians realize, as did Old Tarwater, that they don't tell
their own story — as the modern mythology of freedom would have

it — but rather that they already belong to a Story and that their freedom is authentically discovered in relation to that narrative.

After hearing the Word of God, worshiping Christians perform one of the spiritual works of mercy: they pray for one another, especially for the sick, the needy, and the dead. Rooted together in the divine center, Christians know that they are connected to one another and that they, accordingly, must bear each other's burdens in love. They pray for each other because there is no cell or organ in the body of Christ that functions in isolation. The recitation of prayers on behalf of the weak also serves a very practical function: it lets the community know who is suffering and thus focuses their own exercise of the corporal and spiritual works of mercy.

Signed by the Trinitarian love, aware of their sins, formed by the Word, strengthened as a body, the community is now ready for the properly eucharistic (thanksgiving) phase of the liturgy. We give thanks to God the Father for the gift of his Son by presenting the most precious offering we have: that very gift. After joining our voices, in the great "Holy, Holy," to those of the angels (the heavenly *communio*), we gather around the elements of bread and wine. The priest, acting in the very person of Christ, pronounces the words that Jesus said the night before he died: "take this all of you and eat it; this is my body. Take this all of you and drink from it; this is the cup of my blood." In this inexhaustibly mysterious act, Jesus identifies himself with the elements in such a way that they become the bearers of his very presence. Jesus, crucified and risen, stands in our midst, as he did with the two disciples on the road to Emmaus, as he did with the eleven in the upper room, as he did with Peter and John on the shore of the Sea of Tiberias. The center opens, and we enter in. United with the Son, we become, in him, a sacrifice pleasing to the Father.

The priest then holds up the bread and the cup and says, "Behold the Lamb of God who takes away the sins of the world. How happy are we who are called to this supper." We are meant, not simply to admire the Lamb of God, but to consume him, making him bone of our bone and flesh of our flesh. Jesus said, "I am the vine and you are the branches," and, "Unless you eat the flesh of the Son of Man and drink his blood, you have no life within you," indicating that our relationship to him is organic. Finally, at the climax of the liturgy, we commune with Christ and, in Christ, with one another, solidifying our corporate identity. The social ontology of forgiveness, thanksgiving, and mutual care becomes, in that moment, densely real, not just a hope but an accomplished fact.

At the close of the liturgy, the priest pronounces the simple words, "The Mass is ended. Go in peace to love and to serve the Lord." It has been said that these are, after the words of consecration themselves, the most sacred words of the liturgy. Having visited the center and been formed as the body of Christ, the worshipers are sent out in order to sanctify the world, drawing it into the pattern of what has been realized at the Mass. "Thy kingdom come; thy will be done, on earth as it is in heaven." The *communio* of love which is heaven has been reflected iconically in the *communio* of the eucharistic assembly — and now that icon is meant to be an exemplar to the fallen and dysfunctional world. There is nothing inward-looking or sectarian about the liturgy. As commentators as diverse as Jacques Maritain, Reynold Hillenbrand, Virgil Michel, and Dorothy Day saw, the connection between the Eucharist and social justice is an essential one, since each is the mirror image of the other. A basic conviction of the Christian church is that proper praise of God produces in us a likeness unto God. And thus the liturgy is the practice that fosters a conformity to the Practice which is the Trinity.

And so seeking out the will of God, caring in the most concrete way possible for those around us in need, striving to live in line with the truth of God's nonviolence, iconically displaying the divine life in the liturgy, Christians know that their lives are not about them. In all these ways, they walk the third path.

Concluding Meditation

The Strangest Way

We began with the Buddhist scholar at Gethsemani puzzling over the crucifix and with John the Baptist pointing to the tortured Christ in Grünewald's great painting. Whatever Christianity is, it is something strange. What we have explored in the course of this book are the paths that begin and end with this strange sign, that is to say, with the broken heart of God.

The center that we find (or rather finds us) is the love that connects the Father and Son, the love in which the Father sends and in which the Son is sent, the love manifest on that awful cross. When we had wandered into the cold and distant country of sin, that love came to search us out; when we had sunk under the waves, that love went deeper; when we had closed ourselves up in the somber cave of our self-regard and self-reproach, that love crouched down and, with a candle, entered in. And this is why we Christians don't hide the awful face of the dying Christ. This is why we show it to the world. In Jesus' agonies, God is taking our agony away. In that broken heart, the center opens up.

Thus, in the passion unto death of the Son of God, we see something as beautiful and intricate as Brideshead, as safe and reassuring as Teresa's castle, as intoxicating as Juan de la Cruz's wine cellar, as blissful as Merton's *point vièrge,* as balanced as a rose window at Chartres. In the center which is the Trinitarian love, we can be detached from life and death, poverty and riches, health and disease, fame and disrepute, having no fear of those paper tigers that can only kill the body and do nothing else. Because the divine love has sought us out and brought us in, we start at the top, calling God "Father," and thumbing our noses at Adam, Prometheus, Eve, and the old gods, no longer anxious and upset about many things but focused like a laser on the *unum necessarium*. Rooted in the still point, we accept the fact that we have been accepted, we know that it is no longer we who live but Christ who lives in us, we realize that nothing can ever separate us from the love of God.

Seeking a deeper participation in that center, we practice the first path, walking, like Chaucer's pilgrims, to holy places; praying, like the monks of Mt. Athos, breathing in our redemption and breathing out our rebellion; carrying on our persons, a bit defiantly perhaps, the cross on which hung the salvation of the world; and, like Augustine of the *Confessions*, calming those desires that would distract us from the Desire.

And in the terrible beauty of Christ crucified, we see our own sin. The Lord of Life came and we killed him. Therefore hiding, denying, covering up, pretense, excuses, and subterfuges — all the ruses of self-justification — are permanently out of the question. Our own dysfunction is on public view in every wound on the body of Jesus. When we direct ourselves toward the brilliance of the crucified Christ, every smudge on the window pane of the soul becomes visible: the self-preoccupation that makes ecstasy impossible, the pathetic sadness at the success of a friend, the resentment that rots us like a poison, the laziness of spirit that undercuts the mission, the hunger for everything but the bread of life, the addictions that draw us in on ourselves, the passion that makes of other selves playthings for the ego. In the tormented face of Christ crucified, we know that something has gone terribly wrong with God's creation, that no one is okay, that we are like prisoners chained inside of an escape-proof prison, that we are at war with ourselves, that Pharaoh has enslaved the Israelites and pressed them into service for his purposes, that we are under judgment, that all we can cry is "O Come, O Come, Emmanuel."

But we see something else in the brutality of the cross. We see that God himself has come to stand with us — shoulder to shoulder — in the muddy waters of our dysfunction, that he has absorbed into his forgiveness every single one of the deadly sins, that he has ventured into our slave quarters and shown us the way out, that he has wrestled to the ground the strong man who holds us captive, that he has come to be judged in our place. Yes, we know, with disquieting certitude, that we are sinners, but, with Paul, we willingly boast of our weakness, for we know, with equal clarity, that we are redeemed sinners.

And therefore we walk the second path of holiness, traveling with Merton from side to side and top to bottom of the soul, searching out with the light of redemption all the dark places; walking, like Dante, up an exhilarating *Purgatorio;* confessing, like Augustine, both the stupidity of our sin and the graciousness of our savior; telling, like Martin Luther King, Dorothy Day, Václav Havel, and John Paul II, the truth, the hard and liberating truth; forgiving, like the grief-stricken Amish couple and like the humiliated Cardinal Bernardin, even those who have caused us pain.

In Jesus crucified we also see a mission, embraced from before the beginning of time. The Son of God knows that his life is not about him, but rather consists in doing the will of his Father. Emptying himself, giving himself away, refusing to cling to his prerogatives, the Son is nothing but obedience to a love that generates him. When this Son of God became flesh, the momentum of his obedience carried him where the Father's will wanted him to go: to the limits of godforsakenness, in quest of all of us wanderers, all of us sinners who would prefer just to be left alone. But he wouldn't (and doesn't) leave us alone. He sat down with us in the Hell that our loneliness created. And he continues to sit, waiting us out. At the climax of his mission, he cried out, in anticipation of every missionary who would follow him, "Father, into your hands I commend my spirit." Path three opens up in this awful moment when the Son of God shows us, in a vivid iconic display, that his life is not about him.

To walk this way is to be tied up and taken where we don't want to go. It is to be seized and scarred and frightened; it is to move from the cramped confines of the *pusilla anima* into the new world of the *magna anima;* it is to let go of the pitifully dull ego-drama and to find one's place in the roomy and unpredictable theo-drama; it is to uncover the pearl of great price and the treasure buried in the field of the heart; it is to be young Tarwater, wiping the dirt of great-uncle's grave on his forehead and heading with a message of God's terrible mercy into the city where the children of God lie sleeping; it is to know that the whole cosmos is a conduit and sacrament of the divine providence; it is to sense "the Master's hand in every sparrow fallen, in every grain of sand"; it is to realize that God is not a being among others, not a concept manipulable by the mind, but rather that mystery than which no greater can be thought; it is loving the painting not fully visible, reverencing the book never fully readable, fighting in the army whose victory lies far in the future; it is to live here below as a resident alien, eyes fixed on the true *patria*.

And to walk this third path is to be attentive (eyes, ears, and hearts open) to the slightest movement of grace, to see the biblical forms (Eureka!), to make the awful determination of which way God is clearing, and to have the courage to set out on it. It is to feed that hungry child, to give drink to that thirsty woman, to visit that disagreeable man in prison, to venture into that smelly hospital in search of a lonely child of God, to counsel that teenager lost on the wrong road, to listen out of love to that tedious story, to pray for a soul that no one else remembers. It is to stand in the face of evil, neither flinching nor fleeing, neither fighting nor backing down, stubbornly witnessing that the deepest truth of things is love, magnificently refusing to cooperate with the Father of lies. It is to stand with our brothers and sisters in the midst of the New Jerusalem, realizing here on earth something of the *communio* which is heaven, admitting our sins and opening ourselves to God's glory, listening to the great stories, praying for one another in the fellowship of the saints alive and dead, singing with the angelic chorus, linking our bodies to the broken body and shed blood of the Lamb, and finally going forth to turn the whole world into what we have seen and heard and become.

Dietrich Bonhoeffer commented that when the Lord summons a person to discipleship he calls to him to come and die. When the

blind Bartimaeus received his sight, at the midpoint of the Gospel
of Mark, he followed Jesus up the road that would lead to Calvary.
The way which is the Christian life begins and ends with the man
who is God dying on a cross.

Strange isn't it?

Notes

Introduction: Paths and Practices

1. René Descartes, *Discourse on the Method* in *The Philosophical Works of Descartes*, vol. 1, trans. Elizabeth S. Haldane and G. R. T. Ross (Cambridge: Cambridge University Press, 1979), 88.

2. Ibid., 101.

3. Ibid., 92.

4. Immanuel Kant, *Religion within the Limits of Reason Alone* (New York: Harper and Row, 1960), 139–78.

5. Friedrich Schleiermacher, *The Christian Faith* (Edinburgh: T. & T. Clark, 1989), 76–78.

6. Paul Tillich, *Systematic Theology*, vol. 1 (Chicago: University of Chicago Press, 1967), 10–12.

7. Karl Rahner, *Foundations of Christian Faith: An Introduction to the Idea of Christianity* (New York: Crossroad, 1984), 51–68.

8. Immanuel Kant, "What Is Enlightenment?" in *On History*, ed. Lewis White Beck (New York: Bobbs-Merrill, 1963), 3.

9. Paul Tillich, *Dogmatik: Marburger Vorlesung von 1925,* ed. Werner Schüssler (Düsseldorf: Patmos Verlag, 1986), 37–41.

10. John Henry Newman, *An Essay on the Development of Christian Doctrine* in *Conscience, Consensus and the Development of Doctrine* (New York: Doubleday, 1992), 75.

11. Immanuel Kant, *Foundations of the Metaphysics of Morals* (Indianapolis: Bobbs-Merrill, 1959), 64–72.

12. G. W. F. Hegel, *Lectures on the Philosophy of Religion* in *Hegel Lectures on the Philosophy of Religion: One-Volume Edition, the Lectures of 1827,* ed. Peter C. Hodgson (Berkeley: University of California Press, 1988), 144–54.

13. Quoted in Jakob Laubach, "Hans Urs von Balthasar," *Theologians of Our Time,* ed. Leonhard Reinisch (Notre Dame, Ind.: University of Notre Dame Press, 1964), 146–47.

14. Ludwig Wittgenstein, *Tractatus Logico-Philosophicus* (London: Routledge, 1990), 31–45.

15. Ludwig Wittgenstein, *Philosophical Investigations* (Oxford: Blackwell, 1999), 1–34.

16. See Edward Oakes, *Pattern of Redemption: The Theology of Hans Urs von Balthasar* (New York: Continuum, 1994), 81–88.

17. Thomas Aquinas, *Summa theologiae,* Ia, q. 52, art. 1.

18. William James, *The Principles of Psychology* (Cambridge, Mass.: Harvard University Press, 1983), 948–49.

19. John Henry Newman, *An Essay in Aid of a Grammar of Assent* (Notre Dame, Ind.: University of Notre Dame Press, 1979), 143.

20. Ibid., 234.

21. John Henry Newman, *Fifteen Sermons Preached before the University of Oxford Between A.D. 1826 and 1843* (Notre Dame, Ind.: University of Notre Dame Press, 1997), 257.

22. Thomas Merton, *The Seven Storey Mountain* (New York: Harcourt, Brace, 1948), 264.

Chapter One: Walking the First Path

1. Paul Tillich, *Systematic Theology,* vol. 2 (Chicago: University of Chicago Press, 1967), 178.

2. Thomas Merton, *The New Man* (New York: Noonday Press, 1961), 24–30.

3. See Robert Barron, *And Now I See: A Theology of Transformation* (New York: Crossroad, 1998), 2–6.

4. Evelyn Waugh, *Brideshead Revisited* (Boston: Little, Brown and Co., 1945).

5. Ibid., 28.

6. Ibid., 39.

7. Ibid., 82.

8. Plato, *Symposium* in *Plato: Collected Dialogues,* ed. Edith Hamilton (Princeton: Princeton University Press, 1961), 561–62.

9. James Joyce, *A Portrait of the Artist as a Young Man* in *The Portable James Joyce,* ed. Harry Levin (New York: Penguin Books, 1976), 433.

10. See Hans Urs von Balthasar, *Theo-Drama: Theological Dramatic Theory,* vol. 2: *Dramatis Personae: Man in God* (San Francisco: Ignatius Press, 1990).

11. Waugh, *Brideshead Revisited,* 85–87.

12. Ibid., 102.

13. Ibid., 169.

14. Ibid., 215.

15. Ibid., 309.

16. Ibid., 338.

17. Ibid., 350.

18. Origen, *Homily I on Genesis* in *Origen: Homilies on Genesis and Exodus,* trans. Ronald E. Heine (Washington, D.C.: Catholic University of America Press, 1982).

19. Teresa of Avila, *Interior Castle* (New York: Doubleday, 1961), 28.

20. John of the Cross, *The Spiritual Canticle* in *The Collected Works of St. John of the Cross*, ed. Kieran Kavanaugh (Washington, D.C.: ICS Publications, 1979), 511–18.

21. John of the Cross, *The Ascent of Mount Carmel* in Kavanaugh, *The Collected Works of St. John of the Cross*, 123–24.

22. Ignatius of Loyola, *The Spiritual Exercises of Saint Ignatius of Loyola*, ed. W. H. Longridge, S.S.J.E. (London: A. R. Mowbray, 1955), 26.

23. Anthony de Mello, *The Way to Love: The Last Meditations of Anthony de Mello* (New York: Doubleday, 1992), 9.

24. Augustine of Hippo, *Confessions*.

25. John of the Cross, *The Ascent of Mount Carmel* in Kavanaugh, *The Collected Works of St. John of the Cross*, 68.

26. C. S. Lewis, *The Screwtape Letters* (New York: Simon and Schuster, 1996), 28–29.

27. See Anthony de Mello, *Contact with God: Retreat Conferences* (Chicago: Loyola University Press, 1991), 45–49.

28. Charles Williams, *Essential Writings in Spirituality and Theology*, ed. Charles Hefling (Cambridge, Mass.: Cowley Publications, 1993), 204–30.

29. Geoffrey Chaucer, *Canterbury Tales* (New York: Alfred A. Knopf, 1958), 1.

30. Robert Barron, *Heaven in Stone and Glass: Experiencing the Spirituality of the Great Cathedrals* (New York: Crossroad, 2000), 95–101.

31. George Weigel, *Witness to Hope: The Biography of Pope John Paul II* (New York: HarperCollins, 1999), 680.

32. See, for example, Susan Howatch, *Absolute Truths* (New York: Fawcett Crest, 1994).

33. Matthew Fox, *Confessions: The Making of a Post-Denominational Priest* (San Francisco: Harper Collins, 1996), 18.

34. Pope Leo XIII, *Rerum Novarum*, 21, in *Proclaiming Justice and Peace: Papal Documents from Rerum Novarum through Centesimus Annus*, ed. Michael Walsh (Mystic, Conn.: Twenty-Third Publications, 1994), 25.

35. Mary Douglas, *Natural Symbols: Explorations in Cosmology* (London: Routledge, 1996), 37–53.

Chapter Two: Walking the Second Path

1. G. K. Chesterton, *Alarms and Discursions* (London: Methuen, 1924).

2. John of the Cross, *The Dark Night of the Soul* in *The Collected Works of St. John of the Cross*, ed. Kieran Kavanaugh (Washington, D.C.: ICS Publications, 1979), 344.

3. Robert Barron, *Heaven in Stone and Glass: Experiencing the Spirituality of the Great Cathedrals* (New York: Crossroad, 2000), 21–27.

4. Flannery O'Connor, "Revelation" in *O'Connor: Collected Works* (New York: Viking Press, 1988), 633.

5. Ibid., 637.

6. Ibid., 643.

7. Ibid., 638.

8. Ibid., 644.

9. Ibid., 646.

10. Ibid., 654.

11. Henri de Lubac, *Le mystère du surnaturel*; English trans.: *The Mystery of the Supernatural* (New York: Herder and Herder, 1967), 147.

12. Peter Kreeft, *Christianity for Modern Pagans: Pascal's Pensées* (San Francisco: Ignatius Press, 1993), 47.

13. Blaise Pascal, *Pensées* (London: Penguin Books, 1995), no. 401.

14. Ibid., no. 678.

15. Origen, *Homilies on Genesis and Exodus*, 233–34.

16. Dante, *The Divine Comedy: Inferno, Canto I*, trans. Mark Musa (New York: Penguin Books, 1984), 381.

17. Ibid., 67.

18. Ibid., 70–71.

19. Dante, *The Divine Comedy: Purgatorio, Canto 1, 2*.

20. Helen Luke, *Dark Wood to White Rose: Journey and Transformation in Dante's Divine Comedy* (New York: Parabola Books, 1993), 49.

21. Dante, *The Divine Comedy: Purgatorio, Canto IX*, 99.

22. Ibid.

23. Anthony de Mello, *The Way to Love: The Last Meditations of Anthony de Mello* (New York: Doubleday, 1992), 1–4.

24. De Mello, *The Way to Love*, 3.

25. Dante, *The Divine Comedy: Purgatorio, Canto XIII*, 140.

26. Ibid., 139.

27. Thomas Aquinas, *Summa theologiae*, IIa IIae, q. 158, art. 1.

28. Martin Luther King, "Our God Is Marching On!" in *A Testament of Hope: The Essential Writings of Martin Luther King, Jr.* (San Francisco: Harper and Row, 1986), 230.

29. Thomas Aquinas, *Summa theologiae*, IIa IIae, q. 158, art. 4.

30. Luke, *Dark Wood to White Rose*, 80.

31. Dorothy Sayers, *The Comedy of Dante Alighieri, Cantica II, Purgatory* (London: Penguin Books, 1955), 209.

32. Dante, *The Divine Comedy, Purgatorio, Canto XIX*, 202–6.

33. Thomas Aquinas, *Summa theologiae*, Ia IIae, q. 2, art. 1.

34. Karl Marx, *Economic and Philosophical Manuscripts of 1844*, in *Marx-Engels Studienausgabe Politische Ökonomie* (Frankfurt am Main: Fischer Taschenbuch, 1966), 2:112.

35. Dante, *The Divine Comedy, Purgatorio, Canto XIX*, 204.

36. Ibid., 205.

37. Dante, *The Divine Comedy, Purgatorio, Canto XXIII*, 250.

38. John Henry Newman, "An Essay on the Development of Christian Doctrine," in *Conscience, Consensus and the Development of Doctrine* (New York: Doubleday, 1992), 291.

39. Karol Wojtyla, *Love and Responsibility* (San Francisco: Ignatius Press, 1993), 28–31.

40. C. S. Lewis, *Mere Christianity* (New York: Simon and Schuster, 1996), 51.

41. Hans Küng, *On Being a Christian* (Garden City, N.Y.: Image Books, 1984), 212.

42. Bob Dylan, "Slow Train Coming" from the album *Slow Train Coming,* Columbia Records, 1979.

43. See James Alison, *The Joy of Being Wrong* (New York: Crossroad, 1998), 70–77.

44. Alasdair MacIntyre, *After Virtue* (Notre Dame, Ind.: University of Notre Dame Press, 1984), 23–35.

45. Ignatius of Loyola, *Spiritual Exercises,* 44–52.

46. Thomas Merton, "Fire Watch: July 4th, 1952," in *Entering the Silence: The Journals of Thomas Merton*, vol. 2, 1941–1952 (San Francisco: Harper and Row, 1995), 479.

47. Ibid.

48. Ibid., 480.

49. Ibid., 486.

50. Ibid., 480.

51. William C. Placher, *Unapologetic Theology: A Christian Voice in a Pluralistic Conversation* (Louisville: Westminster/John Knox, 1989), 17–26.

52. John Rawls, *A Theory of Justice* (Cambridge, Mass.: Harvard University Press, 1971), 303.

53. Jürgen Habermas, *The Theory of Communicative Action*, vol. 2, trans. Thomas McCarthy (Boston: Beacon Press, 1987), 46–77.

54. *Casey v. Planned Parenthood of Southeastern Pennsylvania*, 112 Sup. Ct. 2791 at 2807.

55. Stanley Hauerwas and William H. Willimon, *Resident Aliens* (Nashville: Abingdon Press, 1989), 13–132.

56. George Weigel, *Soul of the World* (Grand Rapids: Eerdmans, 1996), 159–60.

Chapter Three: Walking the Third Path

1. See Robert Barron, *And Now I See: A Theology of Transformation* (New York: Crossroad, 1998), 5–9.

174   *Notes to Pages 115–135*

2. Pierre Teilhard de Chardin, *The Divine Milieu* (New York: Harper and Row, 1965), 49–93.

3. Anselm of Canterbury, *Proslogion* in *St. Anselm: Basic Writings* (La Salle, Ill.: Open Court Books, 1974), 1.

4. Ibid., 1–2.

5. Ibid., 7–8.

6. Meister Eckhart, "Sermon 22: Ave, gratia plena," in *Meister Eckhart: The Essential Sermons, Commentaries, Treatises, and Defense* (New York: Paulist Press, 1981), 192–96.

7. Bob Dylan, "Idiot Wind" from the album *Blood on the Tracks*, Columbia Records, 1974.

8. Hans Urs von Balthasar, *Theo-Drama: Theological Dramatic Theory*, vol. 2: *Dramatis Personae: Man in God* (San Francisco: Ignatius Press, 1990), esp. 284–334.

9. Dante, *The Divine Comedy, Paradiso, Canto XXXI*, 365.

10. Hans Urs von Balthasar, *The Office of Peter and the Structure of the Church* (San Francisco: Ignatius Press, 1986), 148–61.

11. See Marva Dawn, *A Royal Waste of Time* (Grand Rapids: Eerdmans, 1999).

12. von Balthasar, *The Office of Peter and the Structure of the Church*, 196–212.

13. Flannery O'Connor, *The Violent Bear It Away*, in *O'Connor: Collected Works* (New York: Viking Press, 1988), 331.

14. Ibid.

15. Ibid., 340.

16. Ibid., 354.

17. Flannery O'Connor, "A Good Man Is Hard to Find," in *O'Connor: Collected Works*, 152.

18. O'Connor, *The Violent Bear It Away*, 388.

19. Ibid., 415.

20. Ibid., 434.

21. Ibid., 438.

22. Ibid., 450.

23. Ibid., 456.

24. Ibid., 477.

25. Ibid., 478.

26. Ibid.

27. Flannery O'Connor, "Letter to John Hawkes," in *O'Connor: Collected Works*, 1108.

28. Stanley Hauerwas, *Sanctify Them in the Truth: Holiness Exemplified* (Nashville: Abingdon, 1998), 197–98.

29. O'Connor, "Letter to A," in *O'Connor: Collected Works*, 1101.

30. Ibid.

31. Robert Barron, *Heaven in Stone and Glass: Experiencing the Spirituality of the Great Cathedrals* (New York: Crossroad, 2000), 47–53.

32. Joseph Ratzinger, *Introduction to Christianity* (San Francisco: Ignatius Press, 1990), 106.

33. Albert Einstein, *Mein Weltbild*, cited in ibid.

34. Ratzinger, *Introduction to Christianity*, 105.

35. See Oliva Blanchette, *The Perfection of the Universe according to Aquinas: A Teleological Cosmology* (University Park: Pennsylvania State University Press, 1992), 42–45.

36. Thomas Aquinas, *Commentary on the Ethics of Aristotle*, lec.1, n. 1.

37. See, for example, Thomas Aquinas, *Summa theologiae*, Ia, q. 66, art. 1, ad 3; Ia, q. 91, art. 3; In Job, ch. 37, p. 125.

38. Dante, *Divine Comedy, Paradiso, Canto XXXIII*, 392.

39. Jean-Pierre de Caussade, *Abandonment to Divine Providence* (New York: Doubleday, 1975), 22–32.

40. Bernard Lonergan, *Method in Theology* (New York: Herder and Herder, 1972), 8–9.

41. Bernard Lonergan, *Understanding and Being*, in *Collected Works of Bernard Lonergan*, vol. 5 (Toronto: University of Toronto Press, 1980), 23–32.

42. John Henry Newman, "On Consulting the Faithful in Matters of Doctrine," in *Conscience, Consensus and the Development of Doctrine* (New York: Doubleday, 1992), 398.

43. Thomas Hobbes, *Leviathan* (New York: Penguin Books, 1980), 183–88.

44. Bob Dylan, "A Hard Rain's Gonna Fall," on *The Freewheelin' Bob Dylan*, Columbia Records, 1963.

45. See John Milbank, *Theology and Social Theory: Beyond Secular Reason* (Oxford: Blackwell, 1990), 422–27.

46. Mohandas K. Gandhi, *Gandhi: An Autobiography: The Story of My Experiments with Truth* (Boston: Beacon Press, 1993), 318–19.

47. Walter Wink, *Engaging the Powers: Discernment and Resistance in a World of Domination* (Minneapolis: Fortress Press, 1992), 175–84.

48. George Weigel, *Witness to Hope: The Biography of Pope John Paul II* (New York: HarperCollins, 1999), 293.

49. "Nevertheless the liturgy is the summit toward which the activity of the Church is directed; at the same time it is the fountain from which all her power flows" (*Constitution on the Sacred Liturgy* [Sacrosanctum Concilium], in *Documents of Vatican II*, ed. Walter Abbott, S.J. [New York: Herder and Herder, 1966], 142).

50. Edward Rice, *The Man in the Sycamore Tree: The Good Times and Hard Life of Thomas Merton* (New York: Image Books, 1972), 97.